The Essential Enneagram

The Essential Enneagram

**The Definitive Personality Test
and Self-Discovery Guide—
Revised and Updated**

David N. Daniels, M.D.
and **Virginia A. Price, Ph.D.**

Originally published as
The Stanford Enneagram Discovery Inventory and Guide

HarperOne
An Imprint of HarperCollinsPublishers

HarperOne

HarperCollins books may be purchased for educational, business, or sales promotional use. For information please write: Special Markets Department, HarperCollins Publishers, 10 East 53rd Street, New York, NY 10022.

HarperCollins Web site: http://www.harpercollins.com

HarperCollins®, ® , and HarperOne™ are trademarks of HarperCollins Publishers.

FIRST HARPERCOLLINS PAPERBACK EDITION PUBLISHED IN 2000

Library of Congress Cataloging-in-Publication Data

    The essential enneagram : the definitive personality test and self-discovery guide / David N. Daniels and Virginia A. Price.
      p. cm.
   ISBN 978–0–06–171316–3
   1. Enneagram.   I. Daniels, David N.   II. Price, Virginia Ann.
  BF698.35.E54E88   2009
  155.2'6—dc22   2009000180

09 10 11 12 13 RRD(H) 10 9 8 7 6 5 4 3 2 1

Contents

Acknowledgments

We greatly appreciate all the individuals who participated in the development of *The Essential Enneagram*, originally published as *The Stanford Enneagram Discovery Inventory and Guide (SEDIG)*, especially the Enneagram teachers who participated in typing hundreds of individuals. Special thanks go to Judy Daniels for her many hours of technical support and encouragement.

Major assistance in writing, formatting, and editing was provided by Peter Enemark, Carolyn M. Dawn, and Kit Snyder. Assistance in technical and data analysis was provided by Ghassan Ghandour and Michael Menke.

Our original publisher, Robb Most of Mind Garden, Inc., provided inspiration and support as well as guidance in design and marketing. We extend our thanks to our publisher, HarperOne, to John Loudon, who helped us move forward with our work; to Terri Leonard, executive managing editor, who encouraged us along the way; to Kris Ashley, for her encouragement, upbeat attitude, and constant availability; to Laura Lee Mattingly and Amanda Wood for their work and support on this updated and revised edition, and to Eric Brandt for encouraging this update and revision.

We used the methods of the Narrative Tradition of Self-Discovery and the substantive way of understanding the Enneagram developed by Helen Palmer. *The Essential Enneagram* is based on the understandings and philosophy of Helen Palmer, whose support, encouragement, and guidance we deeply appreciate. Heartfelt thanks go to my teaching colleagues, Peter O'Hanrahan and Terry Saracino, for their extensive contribution to my understanding of the Enneagram. I am especially grateful to Terry for co-creating the Universal Growth Process with me.

Lastly, I am eternally grateful to my coauthor and friend, Virginia Price, who passed away before this revision and update was envisioned. She remains an inspiration and guide.

David N. Daniels, M.D.

Foreword

The Essential Enneagram offers a groundbreaking and original approach to a key problem in personality study. How do you correctly find your place within a rich and complex system when the choice itself requires knowing yourself beforehand? In bringing their combined talents and deep scholastic commitment to the question of self-identification, David Daniels and Virginia Price have made it a whole lot easier to correctly discover your Enneagram personality profile, thus opening a wealth of information for both psychological and spiritual development.

Their innovative method looks like a guided tour to discovering, confirming, and verifying your personality type. You are provided with key checkpoints along the way to make sure you stay on track, and a set of sensitive, practical exercises to aid your personal development once you've discovered your type. David and Virginia are the first authors to bring both scientific validity and reliability studies to the Enneagram. Their method of determining personality type is based on seven years of research with more than 900 subjects.

In Section 1, they provide you with the user-friendly, short-paragraph test that their subjects used. They next show you the probability that the type you chose is correct, and probabilities are the absolute best that any depth psychometric instrument can provide. You are then shown how to confirm your choice, and exactly what steps to take if this checkpoint leads you to believe you are not the type you originally chose.

Once you're certain of your Enneagram profile, you move ahead to Section 2, where the authors give excellent daily practices that assist you in becoming more consciously aware of how your type is organized, its positive features, and how to break free of the limits your type imposes upon you. *The Essential Enneagram* is based on principles of self-awareness that I have long advocated. By providing elegant and precise descriptions of how different types of people are organized and motivated, this book guides you in exploring how your placement of attention and use of energy focuses your worldview, how you deal with stress and anger, and what you can do to develop yourself and receive support from others.

I first had the pleasure of teaching with David when we initiated the Enneagram Professional Training in 1988, using the panel method of personal inquiry. During our now many years of collaboration, I have consistently experienced his inspired clinical acumen, warmth and care, and profound understanding of human behavior and development. He is perhaps the most personally respected contributor in today's emerging field of Enneagram studies.

Virginia likewise brings extraordinary insight and clinical expertise to this work. For more than twenty years she has pioneered, and authored several works about, the theoretical and practical aspects of modifying type A personality behavior. Her research and clinical experience, her understanding of the theoretical basis of personality function, and excellent writing skills have contributed greatly to this field of study.

The section of this book entitled "What to Do When You Have Discovered Your Type" is rooted in David's and Virginia's extensive clinical experience and their understanding of people from the inside out. Their presentation of general methods for personal change and their type-specific practices are exceptionally valuable.

This long-awaited work is a must for anyone interested in effective communication, compassionate relationships, freedom from the confinement of repetitive behavior, and, ultimately, the freedom to be a complete human being.

Helen Palmer
January 2000
Berkeley, California

The Essential Enneagram

SECTION 1:
How to Discover Your Type

PART 1: THE ESSENTIAL ENNEAGRAM
WHAT IS THE ENNEAGRAM?

The Enneagram is a powerful and dynamic personality system that describes nine distinct and fundamentally different patterns of thinking, feeling, and acting. "Ennea" is Greek for nine, and "gram" means a figure or something written. Hence, the Enneagram personality system is represented by a diagram of a nine-pointed star within a circle. Each of the nine patterns is based on an explicit perceptual filter and associated driving emotional energy. This is congruent with the way our neurons operate according to the interwoven flow of information and energy. These patterns determine what individuals of each personality type pay attention to and how they direct their energy and behavior. Underlying each of the nine patterns is a basic proposition, or belief, about what we need in life for survival and satisfaction.

Each one of us developed one of the nine patterns to protect a specific aspect of the self that felt threatened as our own personality was developing. As you discover your Enneagram personality type, you will discover more about your original whole self. You will also understand more about the unconscious motivation from which you operate.

Discovering your Enneagram personality type can help you learn how to bring positive change into your life. It can help change the way you relate to yourself and others as well as give you a greater understanding of the circumstances and issues facing you. Moreover, it can give you powerful assistance in integrating the personal and spiritual aspects of your life, integration being the linkage of differentiated elements.

What Is *The Essential Enneagram?*

We developed *The Essential Enneagram* as a simple and accurate way for individuals to identify their Enneagram personality type and as a guide for further *personal, professional, and spiritual* development.

The Essential Enneagram Test consists of nine short paragraphs that describe the fundamentals of each of the nine personality types. You administer this test to yourself by reviewing the nine paragraphs and choosing the three paragraphs that seem most like you. Next, you put the three selected paragraphs in order, beginning with the one that is the most like you. This process takes only a short time to complete.

You then proceed with an adventure in self-discovery by following the process described in this book, which guides you through the basic terminology of the Enneagram, the determination of your personality type, a comprehensive description of your type, the key discriminators differentiating each type from every other type, and a series of practices for self-development—including practices tailored specifically to your type.

A distinctive feature of the Essential Enneagram Test is its validation by extensive research. We conducted a validity study of just under one thousand individuals. The results of our research show that the Essential Enneagram Test has a high level of validity and reliability. We have included a summary of this research in appendix B (pages 115 to 116).

By using *The Essential Enneagram* in the way described here, you can discover, confirm, and verify your Enneagram personality type with a high level of confidence. Please bear in mind that the purpose of the Enneagram and this book is not to label you but to aid you in your journey of self-understanding and self-development. Remember that you are a human being that just happens to have a personality structure or type. By knowing your Enneagram personality type, you can become aware of the habits of your personality that limit you, and you can free yourself from those habits.

The Process of Self-Discovery and Self-Development Using *The Essential Enneagram*

The Essential Enneagram will guide you step-by-step through the process of taking the Enneagram personality test, discovering and confirming your correct type and pursuing a path of self-development once you know your personality type. Here we provide an overview of that process. When you have read this overview, keep reading and you will see how to begin.

Taking the Essential Enneagram Test

- First, you will read the Essential Enneagram Test instructions and take the test, which involves reading nine short paragraphs and choosing three of them.
- Then you will turn to page 9 to find out how the paragraphs you chose are linked to the Enneagram types.

Discovering and Confirming Your Correct Type

- The Type Determination pages and the Type Description pages are the two key tools you will use to discover and begin to confirm your type. You will find it useful to read the explanations of both the Type Determination pages and the Type Description pages.
- Then go to the Type Determination pages of the type associated with your first-choice paragraph. The Type Determination pages will guide you to the appropriate Type Description pages and provide instructions on how to confirm your correct type.
- You can further confirm your correct type by referring to the "Summary of Type Discriminators," beginning on page 56.
- The final step is to read "How to Confirm and Verify Your Type" on page 69.

What to Do When You Have Discovered Your Type

- First, read the five general principles that apply to all nine Enneagram types and follow, as desired, the practices based on those five principles.
- Then read and follow the five self-development practices associated with your specific type.

How to Begin

Follow the instructions below and complete the Essential Enneagram Test on pages 5 to 7.

Essential Enneagram Test Instructions

Following are nine paragraphs that describe nine different personality types. None of these personality types is better or worse than any other. Each paragraph is meant to be a simple snapshot of one of the nine Enneagram types. No paragraph is intended to be a comprehensive description of an individual's personality.

1. Read the descriptions and pick the three paragraphs that fit you best. Each of the nine paragraphs may describe you to some degree, but choose the three that seem most like you.
2. Number these paragraphs from 1 to 3, with 1 being the paragraph that seems most like you, 2 the paragraph next most like you, and 3 the third most like you.

In making your selections, consider each paragraph as a whole rather than considering each sentence out of the context of its paragraph. Ask yourself, "Does this paragraph as a whole fit me better than any of the other paragraphs?"

If you find it difficult to choose the three paragraphs most like you, think about which descriptions someone close to you would select to describe you. Because personality patterns are usually most prominent before we begin work on personal development, you may also ask yourself which of these patterns would have best described you before you began any such work.

Recording Your Selections

After reading the paragraphs and selecting the three most like you, record the paragraphs you selected:

First choice: A B C D E F G H I
Second choice: A B C D E F G H I
Third choice: A B C D E F G H I

3. Once you have chosen the three paragraphs and recorded them, turn to page 9 to find out how those paragraphs are linked to the Enneagram types.

Essential Enneagram Test

A. I approach things in an all-or-nothing way, especially issues that matter to me. I place a lot of value on being strong, honest, and dependable. What you see is what you get. I don't trust others until they have proven themselves to be reliable. I like people to be direct with me, and I know when someone is being devious, lying, or trying to manipulate me. I have a hard time tolerating weakness in people, unless I understand the reason for their weakness or I see that they're trying to do something about it. I also have a hard time following orders or direction if I do not respect or agree with the person in authority. I am much better at taking charge myself. I find it difficult not to display my feelings when I am angry. I am always ready to stick up for friends or loved ones, especially if I think they are being treated unjustly. I may not win every battle with others, but they'll know I've been there.

B. I have high internal standards for correctness, and I expect myself to live up to those standards. It's easy for me to see what's wrong with things as they are and to see how they could be improved. I may come across to some people as overly critical or demanding perfection, but it's hard for me to ignore or accept things that are not done the right way. I pride myself on the fact that if I'm responsible for doing something, you can be sure I'll do it right. I sometimes have feelings of resentment when people don't try to do things properly or when people act irresponsibly or unfairly, although I usually try not to show it to them openly. For me, it is usually work before pleasure, and I suppress my desires as necessary to get the work done.

C. I seem to be able to see all points of view pretty easily. I may even appear indecisive at times because I can see advantages and disadvantages on all sides. The ability to see all sides makes me good at helping people resolve their differences. This same ability can sometimes lead me to be more aware of other people's positions, agendas, and personal priorities than of my own. It is not unusual for me to become distracted and then to get off task on the important things I'm trying to do. When that happens, my attention is often diverted to unimportant, trivial tasks. I have a hard time knowing what is really important to me, and I avoid conflict by going along with what others want. People tend to consider me to be easygoing, pleasing, and agreeable. It takes a lot to get me to the point of showing my anger directly at someone. I like for life to be comfortable and harmonious and for others to be accepting of me.

D. I am sensitive to other people's feelings. I can see what they need, even when I don't know them. Sometimes it's frustrating to be so aware of people's needs, especially their pain or unhappiness, because I'm not able to do as much for them as I'd like to. It's easy for me to give of myself. I sometimes wish I were better at saying no, because I end up putting more energy into caring for others than into taking care of myself. It hurts my feelings if people think I'm trying to manipulate or control them when all I'm trying to do is understand and help them. I like to be seen as a warmhearted and good person, but when I'm not taken into account or appreciated I can become very emotional or even demanding. Good relationships mean a great deal to me, and I'm willing to work hard to make them happen.

E. Being the best at what I do is a strong motivator for me, and I have received a lot of recognition over the years for my accomplishments. I get a lot done and am successful in almost everything I take on. I identify strongly with what I do, because to a large degree I think your value is based on what you accomplish and the recognition you get for it. I always have more to do than will fit into the time available, so I often set aside feelings and self-reflection in order to get things done. Because there's always something to do, I find it hard to just sit and do nothing. I get impatient with people who don't use my time well. Sometimes I would rather just take over a project someone is completing too slowly. I like to feel and appear "on top" of any situation. While I like to compete, I am also a good team player.

F. I would characterize myself as a quiet, analytical person who needs more time alone than most people do. I usually prefer to observe what is going on rather than be involved in the middle of it. I don't like people to place too many demands on me or to expect me to know and report what I am feeling. I'm able to get in touch with my feelings better when alone than with others, and I often enjoy experiences I've had more when reliving them than when actually going through them. I'm almost never bored when alone, because I have an active mental life. It is important for me to protect my time and energy and, hence, to live a simple, uncomplicated life and be as self-sufficient as possible.

G. I have a vivid imagination, especially when it comes to what might be threatening to safety and security. I can usually spot what could be dangerous or harmful and may experience as much fear as if it were really happening or just question or challenge the situation and not experience fear. I either tend to avoid danger or tend to challenge it head-on. In fact, sometimes I do not experience much fear since I go into action with little hesitation. My imagination also leads to my ingenuity and a good, if somewhat offbeat, sense of humor. I would like for life to be more certain, but in general I seem to doubt or question the people and things around me. I can usually see the shortcomings in the view someone is putting forward. I suppose that, as a consequence, some people may consider me to be very astute. I tend to be suspicious of authority and am not particularly comfortable being seen as the authority. Because I can see what is wrong with the generally held view of things, I tend to identify with underdog causes. Once I have committed myself to a person or cause, I am very loyal to it.

H. I am an optimistic person who enjoys coming up with new and interesting things to do. I have a very active mind that quickly moves back and forth between different ideas. I like to get a global picture of how all these ideas fit together, and I get excited when I can connect concepts that initially don't appear to be related. I like to work on things that interest me, and I have a lot of energy to devote to them. I have a hard time sticking with unrewarding and repetitive tasks. I like to be in on the beginning of a project, during the planning phase, when there may be many interesting options to consider. When I have exhausted my interest in something, it is difficult for me to stay with it, because I want to move on to the next thing that has captured my interest. If something gets me down, I prefer to shift my attention to more pleasant ideas. I believe people are entitled to an enjoyable life.

I. I am a sensitive person with intense feelings. I often feel misunderstood and lonely, because I feel different from everyone else. My behavior can appear like drama to others, and I have been criticized for being overly sensitive and overamplifying my feelings. What is really going on inside is my longing for both emotional connection and a deeply felt experience of relationship. I have difficulty fully appreciating present relationships because of my tendency to want what I can't have and to disdain what I do have. The search for emotional connection has been with me all my life, and the absence of emotional connection has led to melancholy and depression. I sometimes wonder why other people seem to have more than I do—better relationships and happier lives. I have a refined sense of aesthetics, and I experience a rich world of emotions and meaning.

Important:
Please be sure you have completed
the Essential Enneagram Test
before reading any further.

Linking Paragraphs to Types

Find the types that correspond to each of the paragraphs you chose.

Test Paragraph	Enneagram Type	Type Determination Pages
A	Type 8	Pages 48–49
B	Type 1	Pages 20–21
C	Type 9	Pages 52–53
D	Type 2	Pages 24–25
E	Type 3	Pages 28–29
F	Type 5	Pages 36–37
G	Type 6	Pages 40–41
H	Type 7	Pages 44–45
I	Type 4	Pages 32–33

The Enneagram Figure

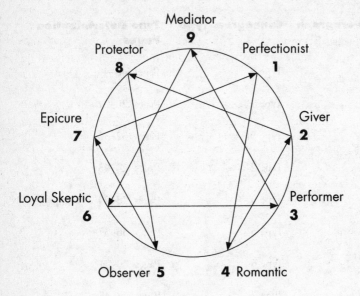

"Ennea" is Greek for nine, and "gram" means figure or something written. The word "Enneagram" then refers to a nine-pointed star that is shown inside a circle.

The arrows on this diagram indicate the stress and security types associated with each Enneagram personality type. The stress type is in the direction of the arrow, and the security type is away from the arrow. See page 14 for an explanation of security and stress types.

How to Proceed

By this time you have taken the Essential Enneagram Test and linked your first-, second-, and third-choice paragraphs to their respective Enneagram types.

Now you are ready to read the explanation of the Type Determination and Type Description pages, which are critical to determining your type. The Type Determination and Type Description pages are the main part of *The Essential Enneagram* guide to personality type. To identify, confirm, and verify your correct type, it is crucial to understand the terminology and format of the Type Determination and Type Description pages.

Understanding the Type Determination Pages

The Type Determination pages tell you what the probability is that the paragraph you selected as your first choice is your correct personality type. It also tells you what the principal alternative possibilities are for your correct type given your first-choice paragraph. This quantitative information will help you determine your correct personality type.

The probabilities that appear on the Type Determination pages were discovered through extensive research conducted on the Essential Enneagram Test. A summary of that research can be found in appendix B (pages 115 to 116).

Figure 1 shows you the layout of the Type Determination pages. A detailed explanation of these pages follows figure 1.

Figure 1—Type Determination Pages Layout

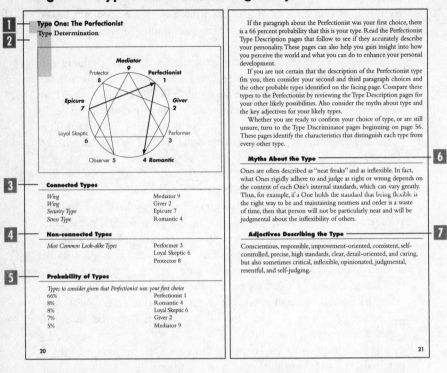

Type One: The Perfectionist
Type Determination

[Enneagram diagram showing:]
- Mediator 9
- Protector 8
- Perfectionist 1
- Epicure 7
- Giver 2
- Loyal Skeptic 6
- Performer 3
- Observer 5
- 4 Romantic

If the paragraph about the Perfectionist was your first choice, there is a 66 percent probability that this is your type. Read the Perfectionist Type Description pages that follow to see if they accurately describe your personality. These pages can also help you gain insight into how you perceive the world and what you can do to enhance your personal development.

If you are not certain that the description of the Perfectionist type fits you, then consider your second and third paragraph choices and the other probable types identified on the facing page. Compare these types to the Perfectionist by reviewing the Type Description pages for your other likely possibilities. Also consider the myths about type and the key adjectives for your likely types.

Whether you are ready to confirm your choice of type, or are still unsure, turn to the Type Discriminator pages beginning on page 56. These pages identify the characteristics that distinguish each type from every other type.

Connected Types

Wing	Mediator 9
Wing	Giver 2
Security Type	Epicure 7
Stress Type	Romantic 4

Non-connected Types

Most Common Look-alike Types	Performer 3
	Loyal Skeptic 6
	Protector 8

Probability of Types

Types to consider given that Perfectionist was your first choice

66%	Perfectionist 1
8%	Romantic 4
8%	Loyal Skeptic 6
7%	Giver 2
5%	Mediator 9

Myths About the Type

Ones are often described as "neat freaks" and as inflexible. In fact, what Ones rigidly adhere to and judge as right or wrong depends on the content of each One's internal standards, which can vary greatly. Thus, for example, if a One holds the standard that being flexible is the right way to be and maintaining neatness and order is a waste of time, then that person will not be particularly neat and will be judgmental about the inflexibility of others.

Adjectives Describing the Type

Conscientious, responsible, improvement-oriented, consistent, self-controlled, precise, high standards, clear, detail-oriented, and caring, but also sometimes critical, inflexible, opinionated, judgmental, resentful, and self-judging.

20   21

---

1 **Enneagram Type** The number and descriptive title of each Enneagram type.

2 **Type Determination** These two facing pages that help you determine which types are likely to be your actual type.

3 **Connected Types** The four personality types that are associated with your basic type.

4 **Non-connected Types** The personality types that most often manifest characteristics similar to your basic type.

5 **Probability of Types** The probability that you might be a type other than the one associated with your first-choice paragraph.

6 **Myths About Type** Stereotypes about the types that lead to false beliefs and to inadvertent rejection of the type.

7 **Adjectives Describing the Type** The adjectives that serve as a useful supplement in determining type.

Detailed Explanation of the Type Determination Pages

The following paragraphs refer to figure 1.

1 Title of Type

The title of each type is self-evident.

2 Type Determination

The first two facing pages for each type are labeled Type Determination because they help you determine if the type you chose as your first choice is your correct type. These pages show the probability that you are in fact your first-choice type. They also show the probabilities that you might be another type—more specifically, the probability that you might be one of the *connected types* or one of the non-connected *look-alike types* associated with your first choice. You might also be your second- or third-choice type.

3 Connected Types

Each Enneagram personality type has four connected types (the two wings and the security and stress types). These are the four personality types associated with each basic personality type according to Enneagram personality theory. The Type Determination pages show the four connected types for each corresponding Enneagram type. Remember that you may be one of the connected types associated with your first choice.

Wings

Two of the connected types are called wings. They are the personality types on either side of your type on the Enneagram diagram. For example, if you are a Performer (Type Three), then the two personality types that are your wings are the Giver (Type Two) and the Romantic (Type Four). If you are the Mediator (Type Nine), then your two wings are the Protector (Type Eight) and the Perfectionist (Type One). According to Enneagram theory, your personality type is influenced by one or both of the personality types that are your wings.

Security Type and Stress Type

The other two connected types are called the security type and the stress type. Your stress type is the personality type you shift into when you feel stressed and pressured or when you are mobilizing for action. *On the Enneagram figure, the stress type is indicated by the direction to which the arrow points.* Your security type is the personality type you shift toward when you feel relaxed and secure or, paradoxically, when you feel overwhelmed or exhausted. *On the Enneagram figure, the security type is the direction away from the arrow.* Each Enneagram type has its own security type and its own stress type. When you shift into your stress type or your security type, you may show either the higher qualities or the lower qualities of that type depending on the circumstances.

Although the existence of connected types influencing your actual personality type tends to complicate the process of identifying your correct type, they also make the Enneagram system of personality a rich and dynamic system and help account for the fact that each of us is unique.

4 Non-connected Types

Non-connected types are personality types on the Enneagram that can bear a definite similarity or even look alike for some reason other than that they are wings or stress or security types. When you choose paragraphs on the Essential Enneagram Test that seem most like you, you may inadvertently choose one of your non-connected look-alike types instead of your actual type. The procedure described on the Type Determination pages will help you discover if a type you choose on the test is your correct personality type or a look-alike of your correct personality type.

5 Probability of Types

Research with the Essential Enneagram Test shows the probability that you are a particular type given the paragraph you selected as your first choice. Each Type Determination section includes a table listing these probabilities. For example, look at page 20, Type One. If one hundred people choose paragraph B as their first choice on the Essential Enneagram Test, then sixty-six of those people will have Type One as their eventual correct type. However, eight of the one hundred people will eventually find that Type Four is their correct type, and another eight will find that Type Six is their correct type. Furthermore, some others will discover that they are one of their lower probability types, either their second or third choice, or a look-alike type.

6 Myths About the Type

Stereotypes develop about each of the types that involve false beliefs about the type. Sometimes this leads to misunderstandings about the type and rejection of the type as the correct type. When you are choosing a type, be sure to include consideration of the false beliefs or misconceptions about the type. Then you will not inadvertently reject this type.

7 Adjectives Describing the Type

These adjectives can help in type determination if most of them describe you, thus pointing to a good fit. Since some are "negative" descriptors, assessing how well they describe you requires being candid and willing to be non-judgmental toward yourself. We all have some "negative" characteristics.

Understanding the Type Description Pages

The Type Description pages provide you with a detailed description of the properties and characteristics of each of the nine Enneagram types. This qualitative information will help you confirm that you have selected your correct personality type. The wealth of information on the Type Description pages will help you understand your type more clearly and thoroughly. These pages also describe the path of personal development for each type.

Figure 2 shows you the layout of the Type Description pages. A detailed explanation of these pages follows figure 2.

Figure 2—Type Description Pages Layout

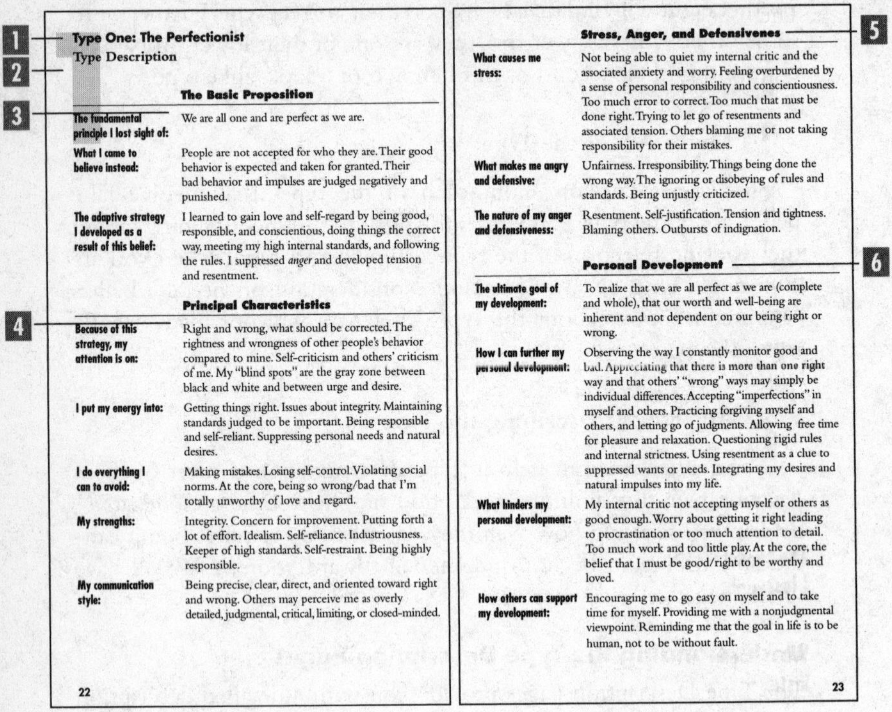

1 → Type One: The Perfectionist
2 → Type Description

The Basic Proposition

3 → **The fundamental principle I lost sight of:**	We are all one and are perfect as we are.
What I came to believe instead:	People are not accepted for who they are. Their good behavior is expected and taken for granted. Their bad behavior and impulses are judged negatively and punished.
The adaptive strategy I developed as a result of this belief:	I learned to gain love and self-regard by being good, responsible, and conscientious, doing things the correct way, meeting my high internal standards, and following the rules. I suppressed *anger* and developed tension and resentment.

Principal Characteristics

4 → **Because of this strategy, my attention is on:**	Right and wrong, what should be corrected. The rightness and wrongness of other people's behavior compared to mine. Self-criticism and others' criticism of me. My "blind spots" are the gray zone between black and white and between urge and desire.
I put my energy into:	Getting things right. Issues about integrity. Maintaining standards judged to be important. Being responsible and self-reliant. Suppressing personal needs and natural desires.
I do everything I can to avoid:	Making mistakes. Losing self-control. Violating social norms. At the core, being so wrong/bad that I'm totally unworthy of love and regard.
My strengths:	Integrity. Concern for improvement. Putting forth a lot of effort. Idealism. Self-reliance. Industriousness. Keeper of high standards. Self-restraint. Being highly responsible.
My communication style:	Being precise, clear, direct, and oriented toward right and wrong. Others may perceive me as overly detailed, judgmental, critical, limiting, or closed-minded.

Stress, Anger, and Defensiveness — **5**

What causes me stress:	Not being able to quiet my internal critic and the associated anxiety and worry. Feeling overburdened by a sense of personal responsibility and conscientiousness. Too much error to correct. Too much that must be done right. Trying to let go of resentments and associated tension. Others blaming me or not taking responsibility for their mistakes.
What makes me angry and defensive:	Unfairness. Irresponsibility. Things being done the wrong way. The ignoring or disobeying of rules and standards. Being unjustly criticized.
The nature of my anger and defensiveness:	Resentment. Self-justification. Tension and tightness. Blaming others. Outbursts of indignation.

Personal Development — **6**

The ultimate goal of my development:	To realize that we are all perfect as we are (complete and whole), that our worth and well-being are inherent and not dependent on our being right or wrong.
How I can further my personal development:	Observing the way I constantly monitor good and bad. Appreciating that there is more than one right way and that others' "wrong" ways may simply be individual differences. Accepting "imperfections" in myself and others. Practicing forgiving myself and others, and letting go of judgments. Allowing free time for pleasure and relaxation. Questioning rigid rules and internal strictness. Using resentment as a clue to suppressed wants or needs. Integrating my desires and natural impulses into my life.
What hinders my personal development:	My internal critic not accepting myself or others as good enough. Worry about getting it right leading to procrastination or too much attention to detail. Too much work and too little play. At the core, the belief that I must be good/right to be worthy and loved.
How others can support my development:	Encouraging me to go easy on myself and to take time for myself. Providing me with a nonjudgmental viewpoint. Reminding me that the goal in life is to be human, not to be without fault.

22   23

1 **Enneagram Type** The number and descriptive title of each Enneagram type.

2 **Type Description** These two facing pages that provide details on the personality type.

3 **The Basic Proposition** Description of the evolution of the personality type and the core beliefs of the type.

4 **Principal Characteristics** Description of the basic characteristics of the strategy that the type has developed.

5 **Stress, Anger, and Defensiveness** Description of the cause and nature of stress and anger for the type.

6 **Personal Development** Key information about personal development for the type.

Detailed Explanation of the Type Description Pages

The following paragraphs refer to figure 2.

▌1 Title of Type

The title of each type is self-evident.

▌2 Type Description

The second two facing pages for each type are labeled Type Description pages because they describe each personality type in detail. These pages also include ideas about how to use knowledge of your personality type for self-development. Each of the Type Description pages follows a logical sequence, beginning with the basic proposition of each type.

▌3 The Basic Proposition

The basic proposition consists of three parts:

The fundamental principle I lost sight of:	A basic truth about life that my early experiences and natural tendencies led me to lose sight of while my personality was forming.
What I came to believe instead:	The core belief that grew out of my early experiences and natural tendencies that caused the original fundamental principle to fade into the background.
The adaptive strategy I developed as a result of this belief:	The adaptive and coping *or* survival strategy I developed because of this core belief in order to preserve a sense of security, love, and worth.

▌4 Principal Characteristics

The second section of the Type Description pages describes the principal characteristics associated with the strategy each type developed.

Because of this strategy, my attention is on:	Whatever is required to support and sustain the particular adaptive and survival strategy of my type, including my "blind spots"—that which is not seen.
I put my energy into:	Whatever is required by my habit of attention, since behavior follows attention and associated emotional energy.

I do everything I can to avoid:	Whatever would threaten the basic adaptive and survival strategy of my type, including my deepest concerns and fears, many of which are unconscious.
My strengths:	The positive qualities that develop out of and are associated with the specific adaptive and survival strategy of my type.
My communication style:	The way my type expresses itself, both positives and negatives.

5 Stress, Anger, and Defensiveness

The third section discusses the stress, anger, and defensiveness associated with each type:

What causes me stress:	The situations and circumstances that cause stress and distress for my personality type.
What makes me angry and defensive:	The specific factors, usually hurt feelings and experienced violations, that evoke anger in my type.
The nature of my anger and defensiveness:	The form that the angry or defensive responses of my type usually takes.

6 Personal Development

The fourth section presents information about personal development for each type.

The ultimate goal of my development:	Recalling and recovering the fundamental principle I lost sight of during the development of my personality.
How I can further my personal development:	The type-specific awareness, steps, practices, and acceptance required to further my personal development (see also "What to Do When You Have Discovered Your Type," which begins on page 71.)
What hinders my personal development:	The specific factors and resistance that impede my personal development, including the core belief that hinders my development.
How others can support my development:	The kind of encouragement and actions of others that are appropriate for my type.

PART 2: HOW TO DISCOVER YOUR TYPE
AND ITS KEY FEATURES

Now turn to the Type Determination pages associated with the Enneagram type that corresponds to your first-choice paragraph. There you will find instructions on how to proceed in discovering your type.

Keep an open mind as you take the steps to discover your type. Try to stay away from premature judgments; that is, wait until after you have read all the Type Description pages of your likely types. While the Essential Enneagram Test is highly accurate, it cannot guarantee that you will correctly select your personality type. Remember that your intuition can be a useful tool to help you know what your correct type is.

Continue your learning by confirming your type for yourself, verifying your type with others, and observing your own thoughts, feelings, and physical sensations. These processes are described in "How to Confirm and Verify Your Type," on page 69, and in "How to Build Self-Understanding," on page 70. You can also learn more about your Enneagram type from the books, tapes, and other Enneagram resources listed in appendix A (pages 111 to 113).

Then begin the work of personal and professional development using the knowledge of your Enneagram type. The section "What to Do When You Have Discovered Your Type" suggests a number of practices that will help you become more aware of how your personality functions, take action to change your habitual behavior, preview and review your progress in self-development, practice application of the "4 As" of the Universal Growth Process, and reflect on the ultimate goal of your development.

Above all, remember that you are more than a personality type: you are also a human being who just happens to have a habit of mind as an adaptive and survival strategy. The Enneagram is about discovering the "box" you are in so that you can get out of the confines of that "box" and become a more whole human being.

Type One: The Perfectionist
Type Determination

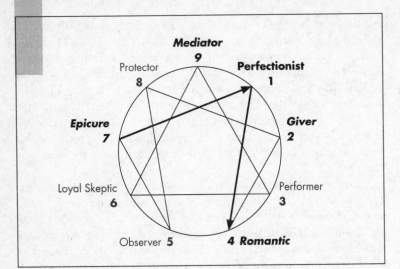

Connected Types

Wing	Mediator 9
Wing	Giver 2
Security Type	Epicure 7
Stress Type	Romantic 4

Non-connected Types

Most Common Look-alike Types	Performer 3
	Loyal Skeptic 6
	Protector 8

Probability of Types

Types to consider given that Perfectionist was your first choice

66%	Perfectionist 1
8%	Romantic 4
8%	Loyal Skeptic 6
7%	Giver 2
5%	Mediator 9

If the paragraph about the Perfectionist was your first choice, there is a 66 percent probability that this is your type. Read the Perfectionist Type Description pages that follow to see if they accurately describe your personality. These pages can also help you gain insight into how you perceive the world and what you can do to enhance your personal development.

If you are not certain that the description of the Perfectionist type fits you, then consider your second and third paragraph choices and the other probable types identified on the facing page. Compare these types to the Perfectionist by reviewing the Type Description pages for your other likely possibilities. Also consider the myths about type and the key adjectives for your likely types.

Whether you are ready to confirm your choice of type, or are still unsure, turn to the Type Discriminator pages beginning on page 56. These pages identify the characteristics that distinguish each type from every other type.

Myths About the Type

Ones are often described as "neat freaks" and as inflexible. In fact, what Ones rigidly adhere to and judge as right or wrong depends on the content of each One's internal standards, which can vary greatly. Thus, for example, if a One holds the standard that being flexible is the right way to be and maintaining neatness and order is a waste of time, then that person will not be particularly neat and will be judgmental about the inflexibility of others.

Adjectives Describing the Type

Conscientious, responsible, improvement-oriented, consistent, self-controlled, precise, high standards, clear, detail-oriented, and caring, but also sometimes critical, inflexible, opinionated, judgmental, resentful, and self-judging.

Type One: The Perfectionist
Type Description

The Basic Proposition

The fundamental principle I lost sight of:	We are all one and are perfect as we are.
What I came to believe instead:	People are not accepted for who they are. Their good behavior is expected and taken for granted. Their bad behavior and impulses are judged negatively and punished.
The adaptive strategy I developed as a result of this belief:	I learned to gain love and self-regard by being good, responsible, and conscientious, doing things the correct way, meeting my high internal standards, and following the rules. I suppressed *anger* and developed tension and resentment.

Principal Characteristics

Because of this strategy, my attention is on:	Right and wrong, what should be corrected. The rightness and wrongness of other people's behavior compared to mine. Self-criticism and others' criticism of me. My "blind spots" are the gray zone between black and white and often to both urge and desire.
I put my energy into:	Getting things right. Issues about integrity. Maintaining standards judged to be important. Being responsible and self-reliant. Suppressing personal needs and natural desires.
I do everything I can to avoid:	Making mistakes. Losing self-control. Violating social norms. At the core, being so wrong/bad that I'm totally unworthy of love and regard.
My strengths:	Integrity. Concern for improvement. Putting forth a lot of effort. Idealism. Self-reliance. Industriousness. Keeper of high standards. Self-restraint. Being highly responsible.
My communication style:	Being precise, clear, direct, and oriented toward right and wrong. Others may perceive me as overly detailed, judgmental, critical, limiting, or closed-minded.

What causes me stress:	Not being able to quiet my internal critic and the associated anxiety and worry. Feeling overburdened by a sense of personal responsibility and conscientiousness. Too much error to correct. Too much that must be done right. Trying to let go of resentments and associated tension. Others blaming me or not taking responsibility for their mistakes.
What makes me angry and defensive:	Unfairness. Irresponsibility. Things being done the wrong way. The ignoring or disobeying of rules and standards. Being unjustly criticized.
The nature of my anger and defensiveness:	Resentment. Self-justification. Tension and tightness. Blaming others. Outbursts of indignation.

Personal Development

The ultimate goal of my development:	To realize that we are all perfect as we are (complete and whole), that our worth and well-being are inherent and not dependent on our being right or wrong.
How I can further my personal development:	Observing the way I constantly monitor good and bad. Appreciating that there is more than one right way and that others' "wrong" ways may simply be individual differences. Accepting "imperfections" in myself and others. Practicing forgiving myself and others, and letting go of judgments. Allowing free time for pleasure and relaxation. Questioning rigid rules and internal strictness. Using resentment as a clue to suppressed wants or needs. Integrating my desires and natural impulses into my life.
What hinders my personal development:	My internal critic not accepting myself or others as good enough. Worry about getting it right leading to procrastination or too much attention to detail. Too much work and too little play. At the core, the belief that I must be good/right to be worthy and loved.
How others can support my development:	Encouraging me to go easy on myself and to take time for myself. Providing me with a nonjudgmental viewpoint. Reminding me that the goal in life is to be human, not to be without fault.

Type Two: The Giver
Type Determination

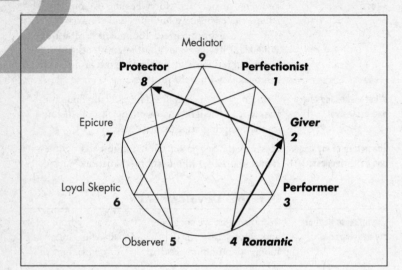

Connected Types

Wing	Perfectionist 1
Wing	Performer 3
Security Type	Romantic 4
Stress Type	Protector 8

Non-connected Types

Most Common Look-alike Types	Epicure 7
	Mediator 9

Probability of Types

Types to consider given that Giver was your first choice

65%	Giver 2
8%	Epicure 7
8%	Mediator 9
7%	Romantic 4
5%	Perfectionist 1

If the Giver paragraph was your first choice, there is a 65 percent probability that this is your type. Read the Giver Type Description pages that follow to see if they accurately describe your personality. These pages can also help you gain insight into how you perceive the world and what you can do to enhance your personal development.

If you are not certain that the description of the Giver type fits you, then consider your second and third paragraph choices and the other probable types identified on the facing page. Compare these types to the Giver by reviewing the Type Description pages for your other likely possibilities. Also consider the myths about type and the key adjectives for your likely types.

Whether you are ready to confirm your choice of type, or are still unsure, turn to the Type Discriminator pages beginning on page 56. These pages identify the characteristics that distinguish each type from every other type.

Myths About the Type

It is often thought that Twos just give to get and underneath are very needy. In fact, Twos often give generously and only appear extra-needy because they repress so much need and desire, making them appear extra "thirsty" or needy.

Adjectives Describing the Type

Caring, helpful, supportive, relationship-oriented, tuned to others' feelings, optimistic, generous, likable, nurturing, advice giving, and responsible, but also sometimes prideful, intrusive, dramatic, often unable to say no, indirect regarding own needs, and over-accommodating.

Type Two: The Giver
Type Description

2

The Basic Proposition

The fundamental principle I lost sight of:	Everyone's needs are equally and freely met in the natural flow of giving and receiving.
What I came to believe instead:.	To get, you must give. To be loved, you must be needed.
The adaptive strategy I developed as a result of this belief:	I learned to get my personal needs fulfilled by being needed and by giving others what I felt they needed and wanted, and I expected that they would then do the same for me. I developed feelings of *pride* in being indispensable.

Principal Characteristics

Because of this strategy, my attention is on:	The needs and wants of others, especially of people I care about and would like to have care about me. Relationships. The moment-to-moment feelings and emotions of others. My "blind spots" are my own needs and my intrusiveness into the lives of others.
I put my energy into:	Sensing the emotional needs of others and doing what pleases them. Feeling good about being able to meet others' needs so well. Creating good feelings in others. Maintaining others' acceptance and approval. Romantic attachment.
I do everything I can to avoid:	Disappointing others. Feeling unappreciated. At the core, being useless and dispensable, hence subject to rejection.
My strengths:	Being giving and helpful. Being generous. Being sensitive to the feelings of others. Being supportive. Being appreciative. Being romantic. High energy. Exuberance. Expressiveness.
My communication style:	Being friendly, open, expressive, focused on others, and quick to support or give advice. Others may perceive me as intrusive, overly helpful, nagging, or controlling.

Stress, Anger, and Defensiveness

What causes me stress:	Feeling needed by so many people and projects. Confusion about my own needs. Being needy myself and having unmet needs. Emotional upheavals resulting from investing so much in relationships, especially challenging ones.
What makes me angry and defensive:	Feeling unappreciated or uncared for. Feeling controlled. Unmet personal needs and wants. People not caring for and supporting others.
The nature of my anger and defensiveness:	Intense, often sudden, emotional outbursts. Saying what others need to give, even blaming others. Crying.

Personal Development

The ultimate goal of my development:	To realize that we are all loved for who we are, not for how much we give or how much we are needed by others. To know that there is a natural flow of giving and receiving.
How I can further my personal development:	Realizing that being loved does not depend on changing myself for others. Gaining clarity about who the real me is and about my own wants and needs. Using anger and rising distress as signals that I am needy. Acknowledging that I am not indispensable and that this is okay. Allowing myself to give and receive without expectations. Practicing setting limits and boundaries on my giving. Noticing when my helpfulness seems intrusive or controlling to others.
What hinders my personal development:	Rationalizations about what I have to do for others before I can do anything for myself. Pride that prevents me from admitting my own needs. Feelings of guilt about being selfish when I pay attention to my needs. Difficulty in receiving from others. At the core, the belief that I am loved and approved based on what I give.
How others can support my development:	Appreciating my independent self instead of being seduced by or dependent on the help I give. Paying attention to my real needs and asking about them. Reinforcing me for saying no when appropriate. Express appreciation for my giving.

Type Three: The Performer
Type Determination

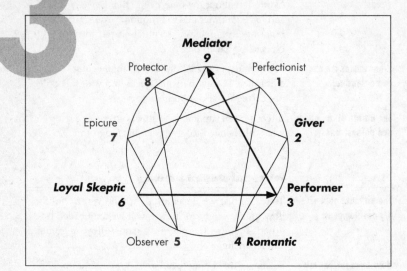

Mediator
9
Protector
8
Perfectionist
1
Epicure
7
Giver
2
Loyal Skeptic
6
Performer
3
Observer 5
4 Romantic

Connected Types

Wing	Giver 2
Wing	Romantic 4
Security Type	Loyal Skeptic 6
Stress Type	Mediator 9

Non-connected Types

Most Common Look-alike Types	Epicure 7
	Perfectionist 1
	Protector 8

Probability Types

Types to consider given that Performer was your first choice

54%	Performer 3
13%	Epicure 7
9%	Perfectionist 1
7%	Giver 2
5%	Protector 8
5%	Mediator 9

If the Performer paragraph was your first choice, there is a 54 percent probability that this is your type. Read the Performer Type Description pages that follow to see if they accurately describe your personality. These pages can also help you gain insight into how you perceive the world and what you can do to enhance your personal development.

If you are not certain that the description of the Performer type fits you, then consider your second and third paragraph choices and the other probable types identified on the facing page. Compare these types to the Performer by reviewing the Type Description pages for your other likely possibilities. Also consider the myths about type and the key adjectives for your likely types.

Whether you are ready to confirm your choice of type, or still unsure, turn to the Type Discriminator pages beginning on page 56. These pages identify the characteristics that distinguish each type from every other type.

Myths About the Type

Threes are often perceived as caring only about their own goals, efficiency, and image, but in fact, Threes can be extremely caring people who bring a positive, can-do attitude to doing for others. In addition, the deceptiveness attributed to Threes is not about deceit, but about being out of touch with their own true feelings, which often are not far from awareness.

Adjectives Describing the Type

Industrious, fast-paced, goal-focused, results- and success-oriented, efficient, confident, enthusiastic, high-energy, caring through doing, ambitious, go-getter, and optimistic, but also sometimes impatient, inattentive to feelings/relationships, competitive, rushed, self-promoting, driven, and overextended.

Type Three: The Performer
Type Description

The Basic Proposition

The fundamental principle I lost sight of:	Everything works and gets done naturally according to universal laws.
What I came to believe instead:	What gets done is dependent on each person's individual effort. People are rewarded for what they do, not for being who they are.
The adaptive strategy I developed as a result of this belief:	I learned to get love and approval by achieving success, by working hard to be the best, and by maintaining a good image. I developed a self-driving, *go-ahead* energy that masked my own true feelings.

Principal Characteristics

Because of this strategy, my attention is on:	All the things that have to be done: tasks, goals, and future achievements. The most efficient solutions. How to be the best. My "blind spots" are failure, deeper feelings, and exaggeration.
I put my energy into:	Getting things done quickly and efficiently. Staying active and busy. Competing. Achieving recognition and credit for accomplishments. Adjusting to whatever is required for success. Promoting myself. Looking good.
I do everything I can to avoid:	Failing to achieve my goals. Being overshadowed by others. Losing face. Experiencing uncomfortable feelings. Having the doubts that can arise from inactivity or from slowing my pace. Dealing with whatever might distract me from getting things done. At the core, being incompetent or incapacitated.
My strengths:	Being personable. Enthusiasm. Leadership. Self-assurance. Being practical, competent, and efficient. Inspiring hope. Poise.
My communication style:	Direct, topic-focused, fast-paced, and confident. Others may perceive me as impatient, unfeeling, overly efficient and restrictive, and overriding of others' views.

Stress, Anger, and Defensiveness

What causes me stress:	The pressure that comes from basing how good I feel about myself on how much I get done and on status, prestige, and power. Not knowing my real feelings and values. Doing too much. Impending failure.
What makes me angry and defensive:	Obstacles: anyone or anything that threatens or thwarts the successful achievement of my goals. Incompetence. Indecisiveness. Inefficiency. Criticism.
The nature of my anger and defensiveness:	Impatience. Irritability. Occasional outbursts.

Personal Development

The ultimate goal of my development:	To realize that love comes from who we are, not what we do, and that everything that needs to be done gets done according to natural laws and does not depend on our individual effort.
How I can further my personal development:	Moderating my pace by practicing patience and allowing things to be as they are. Welcoming in my emotions. Asking myself what really matters. Practicing looking inward for *my* own identity apart from success and the expectations of others. Setting limits and boundaries on work. Allowing myself to listen and be receptive. Developing empathy and understanding. Realizing that love comes from being, not from doing and having.
What hinders my personal development:	Impatience in dealing with my own and others' feelings. Working and overdoing to the point of fatigue and exhaustion. Not slowing down. At the core, believing that love and recognition come from doing, not from being.
How others can support my development:	Encouraging me to pay attention to feelings and relationships. Showing me they care about me for who I am, not for what I have accomplished. Being supportive when I tell them what is really true for me. Letting me know what is really important to them. Reminding me to slow down and smell the roses.

Type Four: The Romantic
Type Determination

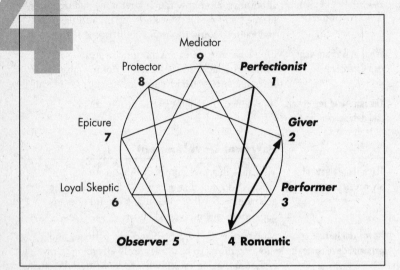

Connected Types

Wing	Performer 3
Wing	Observer 5
Security Type	Perfectionist 1
Stress Type	Giver 2

Non-connected Types

Most Common Look-alike Types	Loyal Skeptic 6
	Mediator 9
	Epicure 7

Probability of Types

Types to consider given that Romantic was your first choice

61%	Romantic 4
11%	Perfectionist 1
7%	Loyal Skeptic 6
7%	Mediator 9
5%	Epicure 7

If the Romantic paragraph was your first choice, there is a 61 percent probability that this is your type. Read the Romantic Type Description pages that follow to see if they accurately describe your personality. These pages can also help you gain insight into how you perceive the world and what you can do to enhance your personal development.

If you are not certain that the description of the Romantic type fits you, then consider your second and third paragraph choices and the other probable types identified on the facing page. Compare these types to the Romantic by reviewing the Type Description pages for your other likely possibilities. Also consider the myths about type and the key adjectives for your likely types.

Whether you are ready to confirm your choice of type, or are still unsure, turn to the Type Discriminator pages beginning on page 56. These pages identify the characteristics that distinguish each type from every other type.

Myths About the Type

Many people believe that Fours are dominated by their feelings and can't be counted upon. In fact, Fours often stay steady despite their strong feelings and accomplish a great deal with dedication as long as they are moved by the activity. They even have a knack for making the ordinary extraordinary.

Adjectives Describing the Type

Idealistic, deeply feeling, sensitive, empathetic, caring, intense, special-ness oriented, creative disposition, authentic to self, introspective, and expressive, but also sometimes dramatic, moody, changeable, self-conscious, unsatisfied, and self-absorbed.

Type Four: The Romantic
Type Description

The Basic Proposition

The fundamental principle I lost sight of:	At the core, everyone has a deep and complete connection to all others and all things.
What I came to believe instead:	People experience a painful loss of their original connections, leaving them feeling abandoned and feeling that they are missing something important.
The adaptive strategy I developed as a result of this belief:	I learned to keep searching for an ideal love or perfect circumstance to make me feel loved, whole, and complete again. I developed feelings of *longing* and *envy* for what was missing.

Principal Characteristics

Because of this strategy, my attention is on:	What is positive and attractive about the future and the past. What is missing or distant that I long for and feel lonely without. What is aesthetic and deeply touching or meaningful. My "blind spots" are what is present and ordinary.
I put my energy into:	A range of intense feelings associated with what seems to be missing or lacking in my life. Finding love, meaning, and fulfillment through self-expression and deep connection. Endeavoring to be a unique individual.
I do everything I can to avoid:	Being rejected, abandoned, not heard, or insignificant. Feeling that I do not measure up. Feeling that there is something wrong with me. The mundane. People and experiences that lack emotional depth. At the core, ending up totally deficient and hence abandoned.
My strengths:	Sensitivity. A creative orientation. Being attuned to feelings. A capacity to empathize with suffering. Intensity. Passion. Romantic idealism. Emotional depth. Authenticity. Introspection.
My communication style:	Expressive of feelings, possibility-oriented, personal, and self-focused. Others may perceive me as overly dramatic, self-absorbed, unsatisfied with responses, and emotionally intense.

Stress, Anger, and Defensiveness

What causes me stress:
People and experiences not living up to my romantic ideals or desire for intensity. Wanting more than is available. Envying what others have that I do not have or what they are that I am not. Unmanageable feelings, especially in emotional crises.

What makes me angry and defensive:
People who disappoint me, let me down, or leave me. Remembering such people from my past. Being slighted, rejected, or abandoned. Feeling misunderstood. Phoniness and insincerity. Not being treated as special or unique. Repeatedly feeling unfulfilled.

The nature of my anger and defensiveness:
Fiery outbursts, sinking into emotion or dissolving into tears. Depression.

Personal Development

The ultimate goal of my development:
To realize that in the present moment we are loved and completely whole, lacking no essential quality or ingredient, and that we are interconnected and at one with all life.

How I can further my personal development:
Focusing on what is positive in life right now rather than on what is missing. Maintaining a consistent course of action despite fluctuating and intense feelings. Cultivating happiness in others in order to become less self-absorbed. Delaying reactive action until intense emotions begin to subside. Appreciating ordinary everyday experiences. Disidentifying self-esteem from specialness and the extraordinary.

What hinders my personal development:
Letting my strong feelings run the show and falling into inaction. Resisting changing "who I am" for fear of losing my individuality. Feeling that I won't measure up. Feeling that the world will let me down. Getting self-absorbed. Downplaying improvement that is not dramatic and becoming discouraged. At the core, believing that I must be and find the ultimate ideal in order to be loved.

How others can support my development:
Encouraging me to keep my attention on what is positive in the present. Honoring my feelings and my idealism. Revealing their real feelings and true reactions. Letting me see that they really understand me instead of trying to change me.

Type Five: The Observer
Type Determination

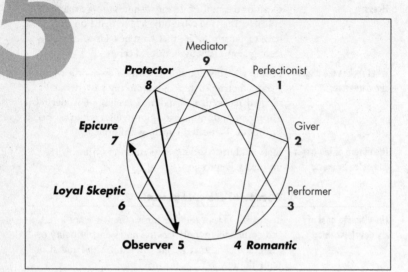

Connected Types

Wing	Romantic 4
Wing	Loyal Skeptic 6
Security Type	Protector 8
Stress Type	Epicure 7

Non-connected Types

Most Common Look-alike Types	Perfectionist 1
	Mediator 9

Probability of Types

Types to consider given that Observer was your first choice

65%	Observer 5
11%	Loyal Skeptic 6
11%	Mediator 9

If the Observer paragraph was your first choice, there is a 65 percent probability that this is your type. Read the Observer Type Description pages that follow to see if they accurately describe your personality. These pages can also help you gain insight into how you perceive the world and what you can do to enhance your personal development.

If you are not certain that the description of the Observer type fits you, then consider your second and third paragraph choices and the other probable types identified on the facing page. Compare these types to the Observer by reviewing the Type Description pages for your other likely possibilities. Also consider the myths about type and the key adjectives for your likely types.

Whether you are ready to confirm your choice of type, or are still unsure, turn to the Type Discriminator pages beginning on page 56. These pages identify the characteristics that distinguish each type from every other type.

Myths About the Type

Some people believe that Fives are not giving, truly stingy, and overly reserved. But Fives are not stingy so much as unwilling to be sharing of self when they experience too many emotional claims or intrusions. Indeed, Fives can be very giving and engaged. They just want to know the extent of the claims on their time and energy, to know the parameters, so to speak.

Adjectives Describing the Type

Self-sufficient, undemanding, quietly caring, knowledgeable, investigative, inquisitive, objective, systematic, analytic, thoughtful, good in a crisis, and unobtrusive, but also sometimes withholding, non-sharing, detached, unassertive, remote, miserly with feelings, and overly private.

Type Five: The Observer
Type Description

The Basic Proposition

The fundamental principle I lost sight of:	There is an ample supply of all the knowledge and energy everyone needs.
What I came to believe instead:	The world demands too much from people and/or gives them too little, potentially leaving them depleted.
The adaptive strategy I developed as a result of this belief:	I learned to protect myself from intrusive demands and being drained of my resources by becoming private and self-sufficient. I did this by limiting my desires and wants and by accumulating a lot of knowledge. I developed a sense of *avarice*, but only for things I could not do without.

Principal Characteristics

Because of this strategy, my attention is on:	The intellectual domain. Facts. Analysis and compartmentalized thinking. Intrusions or demands on me. My "blind spots" are abundance, self-deprivation, and natural support from others.
I put my energy into:	Retracting in order to observe. Learning all there is to know about a subject. Thinking and analyzing in advance. Dampening and reducing feelings. Remaining self-contained to conserve energy. Maintaining sufficient privacy, boundaries, and limits.
I do everything I can to avoid:	Strong feelings, including my own, especially fear. Intrusive or demanding people or circumstances. Feelings of inadequacy and emptiness. At the core, ending up totally drained or depleted and hence unable to cope with life.
My strengths:	Scholarliness. Being knowledgeable. Thoughtfulness. Calmness in crisis. Being respectful. Keeping confidences. Dependability. Appreciation of simplicity.
My communication style:	Content-focused, unemotional, factual, clear, analytical, and terse yet sometimes wordy. Others may perceive me as emotionally disconnected, aloof, overanalytical, or distant.

Stress, Anger, and Defensiveness

What causes me stress:	Failing to maintain sufficient privacy, boundaries, and limits. Becoming fatigued. Having desires, needs, and wants that lead to dependency. Trying to learn everything there is to know before taking action. Too much emotion.
What makes me angry and defensive:	Being considered factually incorrect. Demands, intrusions. Too much emotional input. Not having enough private time to restore my energy.
The nature of my anger and defensiveness:	Self-containment and withholding or withdrawing. Tension and disapproval. Short bursts of temper.

Personal Development

The ultimate goal of my development:	To realize that there is a natural and sufficient supply of what is needed to support and sustain life and that staying engaged in life will provide resources, nurturance, and energy.
How I can further my personal development:	Allowing myself to experience feelings instead of detaching and retreating into my mind. Recognizing that withdrawing and withholding invite intrusion. Taking action in the realization that I have ample energy and support to carry it off, consequently practicing abundance. Finding ways to engage in conversation, to express myself, and to reveal personal matters. Practicing not needing to know.
What hinders my personal development:	Minimizing needs and detaching from the ongoing flow of life. Missing opportunities to do things with others. Isolating myself from my feelings and from connecting with others. Not recognizing fear or anger in myself. Being reluctant to discuss and reveal personal matters. Being excessively analytical. At the core, believing that I must protect myself from depletion in a world that takes too much and gives too little.
How others can support my development:	Respecting my need for privacy and space. Making clear distinctions between their requests and their demands. Providing moderate feedback about their own feelings and concerns. Encouraging me to be self-disclosing and to express my feelings in the here and now. Appreciating my sensitivity. Appreciating my ability to live and let live.

Type Six: The Loyal Skeptic
Type Determination

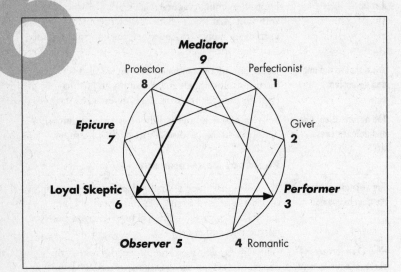

Connected Types

Wing	Observer 5
Wing	Epicure 7
Security Type	Mediator 9
Stress Type	Performer 3

Non-connected Types

Most Common Look-alike Types	Romantic 4
	Protector 8

Probability of Types

Types to consider given that Loyal Skeptic was your first choice

66%	Loyal Skeptic 6
8%	Observer 5
8%	Mediator 9
5%	Romantic 4
5%	Epicure 7

If the Loyal Skeptic paragraph was your first choice, there is a 66 percent probability that this is your type. Read the Loyal Skeptic Type Description pages that follow to see if they accurately describe your personality. These pages can also help you gain insight into how you perceive the world and what you can do to enhance your personal development.

If you are not certain that the description of the Loyal Skeptic type fits you, then consider your second and third paragraph choices and the other probable types identified on the facing page. Compare these types to the Loyal Skeptic by reviewing the Type Description pages for your other likely possibilities. Also consider the myths about type and the key adjectives for your likely types.

Whether you are ready to confirm your choice of type, or are still unsure, turn to the Type Discriminator pages beginning on page 56. These pages identify the characteristics that distinguish each type from every other type.

Myths About the Type

According to some people, Sixes are shrinking violets, pessimistic, and non-trusting. In fact, Sixes often face hazards and difficulties fearlessly to prove themselves capable. Far from being pessimistic, they mostly find positive solutions to the hazards they experience in life. And they can be very trusting and trustworthy as they gain confidence in another person or a situation.

Adjectives Describing the Type

Trustworthy, loyal, responsible, inquisitive, dutiful, good friend, caring, collaborative, analytical, and persevering, but also sometimes overly doubtful or skeptical, uncertain, worrying, vigilant, sometimes challenging and/or fearful, either overly cautious or overly risk-taking, and questioning to the point of blame

Type Six: The Loyal Skeptic
Type Description

The Basic Proposition

The fundamental principle I lost sight of:	We all begin with faith in ourselves, in others, and in the universe.
What I came to believe instead:	The world is unpredictable and hazardous, hence people often can't trust one another.
The adaptive strategy I developed as a result of this belief:	I developed one of two strategies to seek security and certainty as a substitute for basic trust and to avoid feeling fear. *Phobic or accommodating stance:* While I became doubting, vigilant, and questioning, I also learned to obey authority and to avoid perceived threats and hazards. *Counterphobic or challenging stance:* While I became doubting, vigilant, and questioning, I also learned to defy authority and to battle perceived threats and hazards.

Principal Characteristics

Because of this strategy, my attention is on:	What could go wrong or be hazardous. Potential pit-falls, difficulties, incongruities. Implications, inferences, and hidden meanings. My "blind spots" are magnification of hazards and negatives and initially not seeing positives.
I put my energy into:	Doubting, testing, and looking for double messages. Figuring things out through logical analysis. Playing the devil's advocate. Showing strength. Gaining security by obtaining the goodwill of others, being loyal to others, and dedicating myself to worthy and often underdog causes.
I do everything I can to avoid:	Being helpless or not in control in the face of danger and harm. Succumbing to danger or harm. Getting stuck in doubt and contrary thinking. Alienating people I depend on by contradicting or opposing them. At the core, ending up dependent and helpless.
My strengths:	Trustworthiness. Loyalty. Thoughtfulness. Questioning mind. Warmth. Perseverance. Responsibility. Protectiveness. Intuition. Wit. Sensitivity.
My communication style:	Rapid or hesitant, thoughtful to the point of over-explaining, questioning/doubting, engaging yet often

contrary, and information-oriented. Others this may perceive me as overly concerned, challenging, doubting, controlling, and at times pessimistic.

Stress, Anger, and Defensiveness

What causes me stress:
The pressure I put on myself in my efforts to deal with uncertainty and insecurity. Difficulties with authority. Trying to maintain the trust and goodwill of others while experiencing mistrust and ambivalence toward them.

What makes me angry and defensive:
Untrustworthiness, betrayal. Feeling cornered, controlled, or pressured. Interactions with others that feel too demanding. Authorities I can't count on. Others' lack of responsiveness to me.

The nature of my anger and defensiveness:
Wit. Sarcasm. Biting remarks. Accusations. Defensive lashing out.

Personal Development

The ultimate goal of my development:
To realize that it is natural to have faith in ourselves and in one another and that we can embrace and support life without doubt and mistrust.

How I can further my personal development:
Being and acting as my own authority. Reclaiming faith in myself, others, and the universe. Accepting that some uncertainty and insecurity is a natural part of life. Checking out my fears and concerns with others. Recognizing that staying busy is a way to reduce awareness of anxiety. Recognizing that both fight and flight are reactions to fear. Moving ahead with positive action in spite of the presence of fear and thus cultivating courage.

What hinders my personal development:
Doubt and ambivalence. Wanting too much certainty. Being overly controlling or overprotective. Disbelief in my own capacities and decisions. Letting worst-case scenarios dominate my thinking. At the core, believing I must gain certainty and security in a hazardous world that just can't be trusted.

How others can support my development:
Being consistent and trustworthy with me. Being self-disclosing and encouraging me to be self-disclosing. Countering my doubts and fears with positive and reassuring alternatives that are realistic.

Type Seven: The Epicure
Type Determination

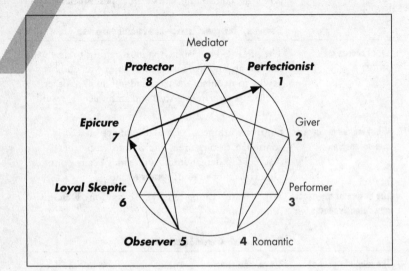

Connected Types

Wing	Loyal Skeptic 6
Wing	Protector 8
Security Type	Observer 5
Stress Type	Perfectionist 1

Non-connected Types

Most Common Look-alike Types	Giver 2
	Performer 3
	Mediator 9

Probability of Types

Types to consider given that Epicure was your first choice

52%	Epicure 7
8.5%	Protector 8
7%	Giver 2
7%	Observer 5
7%	Loyal Skeptic 6
6%	Mediator 9
5.5%	Perfectionist 1

44

If the Epicure paragraph was your first choice, there is a 52 percent probability that this is your type. Read the Epicure Type Description pages that follow to see if they accurately describe your personality. These pages can also help you gain insight into how you perceive the world and what you can do to enhance your personal development.

If you are not certain that the description of the Epicure type fits you, then consider your second and third paragraph choices and the other probable types identified on the facing page. Compare these types to the Epicure by reviewing the Type Description pages for your other likely possibilities. Also consider the myths about type and the key adjecties for your likely types.

Whether you are ready to confirm your choice of type or are still unsure, turn to the Type Discriminator pages beginning on page 56. These pages identify the characteristics that distinguish each type from every other type.

Myths About the Type

Many people believe that Sevens can't keep commitments and try to get out of difficult or trying situations. In fact, Sevens can sometimes end up staying in relationships that are not good for either person because they can always see the positive possibilities. And when something means a lot to Sevens, they can be counted on to stick with a situation or job and to make personal sacrifices and commitments to do so.

Adjectives Describing the Type

Optimistic, upbeat, charming, caring, exuberant, spontaneous, versatile, joyful, possibility- and pleasure-seeking, synthesizer of ideas, opportunity-oriented, quick thinker, and adventurous, but also sometimes pain-avoidant, inconsiderate, unfocused, uncommitted, impetuous, authority-rejecting, and self-serving.

Type Seven: The Epicure
Type Description

The Basic Proposition

The fundamental principle I lost sight of:	Life is a full spectrum of possibilities to be experienced freely and with sustained concentration.
What I came to believe instead:	The world limits people, frustrates them, and causes them pain that can be avoided.
The adaptive strategy I developed as a result of this belief:	I learned to protect myself from limitations and pain by engaging in pleasurable activities and by imagining many fascinating possibilities for the future. I became a *glutton* for interesting ideas and experiences.

Principal Characteristics

Because of this strategy, my attention is on:	Interesting, pleasurable, and fascinating ideas, plans, options, or projects. The interconnections and inter-relationships among diverse areas of information and knowledge. What I want. My "blind spots" are actual limits and the "dark side" of life.
I put my energy into:	Enjoying and experiencing life to its fullest. Keeping options open and life upbeat. Using my active imagination. Being liked by being charming and disarming. Maintaining a privileged position.
I do everything I can to avoid:	Frustrations, constraints, and limitations. Painful situations or feelings. Boredom. At the core, ending up trapped in suffering and pain.
My strengths:	Playfulness. Inventiveness. Being enjoyable and upbeat. High energy. Optimism. Love of life. Vision. Enthusiasm. Helpfulness. Imagination.
My communication style:	Exuberant, fast-paced, spontaneous, analytical, and idea- and possibility-oriented. Others may perceive me as overly quick to shift topics, self-oriented (indifferent to others' input), changeable, and prone to making excuses.

Stress, Anger, and Defensiveness

What causes me stress: Coping with the overload that results from trying to sample all that life has to offer. Making the same mistakes over and over because of my desire to avoid pain. Making commitments and then feeling trapped by them.

What makes me angry and defensive: Constraints or limits that prevent me from getting what I want. People who are stuck, unhappy, depressed, or inclined to blame others, especially if they attempt to drag me down.

The nature of my anger and defensiveness: Brief and to the point. Short-lived. Episodic. Impetuous. Put-downs of others. Acting entitled and superior.

Personal Development

The ultimate goal of my development: To realize that in order to experience life fully we must be consciously present in the here and now and that we support and sustain ourselves and others by cultivating this conscious presence.

How I can further my personal development: Noticing when my quest for pleasurable options is a response to fear of deprivation, a desire to escape from responsibilities that constrain my freedom, or an escape from pain. Practicing working on one thing at a time until it is completed. Living life more fully in the present moment and less in the future. Appreciating more deeply the feelings and concerns of others and practicing loving-kindness. Realizing that it is limiting to seek just the positive and to avoid pain, loss, and suffering. Making and keeping commitments to self and others.

What hinders my personal development: A preoccupation with myself and what I want. Difficulty acknowledging anything negative about myself. Unwillingness to take steps that involve pain or conflict. Being easily distracted and diverted from deeper purposes and commitments. At the core, believing that to ensure a good life I must keep my spirits up and avoid pain and suffering.

How others can support my development: Supporting me when I slow down and stick with my commitments. Letting me know what and how important their own needs and wants are. Encouraging me to deal with pain, fear, and restlessness rather than escaping from these feelings. Helping me keep things simple and in the present.

Type Eight: The Protector
Type Determination

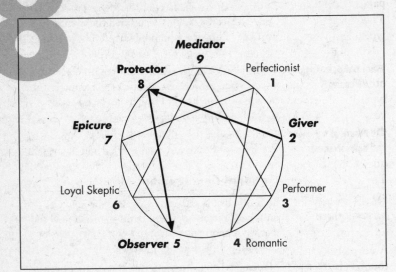

Connected Types

Wing	Epicure 7
Wing	Mediator 9
Security Type	Giver 2
Stress Type	Observer 5

Non-connected Types

Most Common Look-alike Types	Perfectionist 1
	Romantic 4
	Loyal Skeptic 6

Probability of Types

Types to consider given that Protector was your first choice

37%	Protector 8
16.5%	Loyal Skeptic 6
16%	Perfectionist 1
8%	Romantic 4
7%	Epicure 7
6%	Mediator 9

If the Protector paragraph was your first choice, there is a 37 percent probability that this is your type. Read the Protector Type Description pages that follow to see if they accurately describe your personality. These pages can also help you gain insight into how you perceive the world and what you can do to enhance your personal development.

If you are not certain that the description of the Protector type fits you, then consider your second and third paragraph choices and the other probable types identified on the facing page. Compare these types to the Protector by reviewing the Type Description pages for your other likely possibilities. Also consider the myths about type and the key adjectives for your likely types.

Whether you are ready to confirm your choice of type or are still unsure, turn to the Type Discriminator pages beginning on page 56. These pages identify the characteristics that distinguish each type from every other type.

Myths About the Type

A common perception is that Eights are just "out there"—aggressive, tough, and excessive. In fact, Eights can be quite reserved and quiet as well as very giving, generous, and kindhearted, in part because of Eights' all-or-nothing style of relating, but also in women because of the cultural mandate to tame their assertiveness.

Adjectives Describing the Type

Justice-seeking, direct, strong, magnanimous, declarative, assertive, self-reliant, confident, intense, protective of others, and take-charge- and action-oriented, but also sometimes heavy-handed, intimidating, excessive, demanding, impatient, dominating, and impulsive.

Type Nine: The Mediator
Type Description

The Basic Proposition

The fundamental principle I lost sight of:	Everyone belongs equally in a state of unconditional love and union.
What I came to believe instead:	The world makes people unimportant and/or requires them to blend in, making comfort and belonging a substitute for love and worth.
The adaptive strategy I developed as a result of this belief:	Though *inertia* toward my own self and priorities, I forgot myself and merged with others. I substituted inessentials and small comforts for my real priorities as a substitute for unconditional love.

Principal Characteristics

Because of this strategy, my attention is on:	Others' agendas, requests, and demands. All the things in the environment that beckon. My "blind spots": my own position, importance, and priorities.
I put my energy into:	Being sensitive to others and trying to please them instead of myself. Keeping life comfortable and familiar. Maintaining harmony, structure, and routine to make life predictable. Containing anger. Doing the less essential and comforting activities rather than the more important and more disturbing ones.
I do everything I can to avoid:	Conflict, confrontation, feeling uncomfortable. Too many competing demands on my attention and energy. At the core, ending up dismissed as not worth keeping.
My strengths:	Attentiveness to others. Empathy. Supportiveness. Accountability. Steadfastness. Adaptability. Being accepting. Receptiveness. Being caring.
My communication style:	Steady/easygoing, non-confrontational, amiable/friendly, other-directed or focused, and inclusive of both feelings and facts. To others this may be perceived as avoiding conflict, indecisive, rambling, over-explaining, and unclear about own position and role.

wing are the shared characteristics and key discriminators for pair of *connected* and *non-connected* types on the Enneagram, -six in all. The connected types are those that share a wing each other or that have a security-stress connection. Non-cted types often share certain characteristics that can make look alike too.

he two types are *wings.*

he types are *security and stress* types of each other.

he two types are non-connected types that can look alike.

ypes One and Two. Perfectionists and Givers look alike because, wings of each other, they possess some of the same personal-y traits. Both can have high standards of giving, focus intense nergy on the improvement or well-being of others, and know what is best for others. Both types definitely suppress or repress heir own needs and desires. **They differ in that Perfection-sts concentrate, often inflexibly, on others' needs based on heir own inner standards, while Givers, in their focus on •thers' needs, often alter themselves in order to make oth-rs happy. Although both types strive for self-sufficiency nd independence, Givers are very relationship-oriented and •ften find themselves overconnected and even indispens-ble to others.**

Types One and Three. Perfectionists and Performers can be con-idered look-alike types because they are both achievers. Both can •e goal-oriented, competency-oriented, and success-oriented with vorkaholic tendencies. **The differences are that Perfectionists re more likely to be hounded by their inner critic, which notivates them to do what is judged right by the high tandards of the critic, while Performers are more driven o succeed and to change their image and approach, even :utting corners if necessary, to get to the goal and be rec-•gnized for their accomplishments.**

What causes me stress:	Taking a position. Saying no to [...] that person get angry. Having t[...] and set priorities. Dealing with [...] that I didn't really want to mak[...]
What makes me angry and defensive:	Being treated as not important [...] others. Being forced into facin[...] making decisions.
The nature of my anger and defensiveness:	Passive aggression, manifested as [...] resistance. Occasionally "boiling[...]

Personal Development

The ultimate goal of my development:	To realize that we all are uncon[...] loved (accepted and appreciated [...] that our worth and well-being [...]
How I can further my personal development:	Paying attention to my own ne[...] Using anger/resistance as a signa[...] and that something inside me m[...] feelings I may be blocking out [...] real priorities to substitutes, suc[...] or chores. Noticing when my r[...] from setting priorities and takin[...] Accepting discomfort and chan[...] life. Practicing loving myself kin[...] loving others.
What hinders my personal development:	Feeling that I don't count. Feelin[...] deserve to pursue my own agend[...] equal importance and, conseque[...] real priorities. Avoiding the disc[...] required for change. At the core[...] valued and loved I must blend i[...] get along.
How others can support my development:	Encouraging me to express my o[...] me what I want and what is good[...] me time to figure out the answer[...] when I act responsibly toward mys[...] acknowledge my anger. Encourag[...] keep my own boundaries, limits, [...]

S **Types One and Four.** Perfectionists and Romantics share some personality traits because the Perfectionist is the security type of the Romantic and the Romantic is the stress type of the Perfectionist. Both often express idealism, intensity, sensitivity, integrity, authenticity, self-reproach, and a concern for self-improvement. Perfectionists in stress become discouraged and feel deficient. Romantics in security can express a critical idealism and demand perfection or exactness. **They differ in that Perfectionists' idealism concerns correct behavior and "getting it right," while Romantics' idealism revolves around possibilities for ultimate fulfillment. Furthermore, Perfectionists generally are self-restrained, suppressing personal desires, while Romantics experience strong longings and desires, sometimes to the point of self-absorption. Perfectionists cannot express their desires as readily as Romantics do.**

L **Types One and Five.** Perfectionists and Observers can be considered look-alike types because they both are intellectual, competency-oriented, and can become retracted or internalized when trying to figure things out. **Perfectionists, however, are quite intense, suppress their desires, and seek to improve themselves and others, while Observers detach from feelings in order to protect themselves from being intruded upon and to conserve energy. In general, Observers have "a live-and-let-live" attitude and restrict their judgments to intellectual matters, knowledge, and competence, while Perfectionists' judgments extend to the entire range of human activity covered by their internal standards of right and wrong.**

L **Types One and Six.** Perfectionists and Loyal Skeptics can be considered look-alike types because both types can be very watchful, anxious and worried, and intent on figuring things out. **What distinguishes these two look-alike types is that Loyal Skeptics, by doubting, try to figure out what could go wrong, what the worst-case scenario might be, and how to gain a sense of safety and certainty. Perfectionists, by judging and comparing, try to figure out how to prevent mistakes, how to correct what is wrong, and how to avoid self-criticism and criticism from others. Perfectionists' one right way brings clarity, while the doubting and questioning mind of Loyal Skeptics hinders clarity.**

S **Types One and Seven.** Perfectionists and Epicures possess some traits in common because the Perfectionist is the stress type of the Epicure and the Epicure is the security type of the Perfectionist. Both are idealists who want a better world, who show intensity and helpfulness, and who value self-reliance. Perfectionists feeling secure often release themselves from their feelings of responsibility, relaxing into pleasure, personal desire, and playfulness. Epicures in stress can become quite critical, exacting, and determined. **However, while Perfectionists do not seek pleasure and are quite austere, Epicures definitely do seek pleasure and are even hedonistic. Thus, Perfectionists are serious and self-restrained and limit their desires. In contrast, Epicures are fun-loving and expansive and spurn limits.**

L **Types One and Eight.** Perfectionists and Protectors can be considered look-alike types because both are Body Center types (see pages 74–75) and are concerned with rightness, justice, truth, and fairness. **Protectors, however, state their truth openly, express their anger directly, and go from impulse to action easily. Perfectionists suppress anger and impulse, becoming resentful and tense until a sense of righteousness allows their anger to spill out.**

W **Types One and Nine.** Perfectionists and Mediators look alike because as wings of each other and as Body Center types (see pages 74–75) they share some of the same personality traits. They easily forget or suppress their own needs and desires. They value steadiness, organization, and routine, and they work hard for others with care and a concern for harmony. **However, Perfectionists hold to their positions and standards, often rigidly, wanting others to change, while Mediators readily adapt and accommodate to others' positions, often losing sight of their own. Thus, Perfectionists appear tense and press for change, while Mediators go along with the agendas of others, adapting more readity to their requests and claims.**

W **Types Two and Three.** Givers and Performers look alike because as wings of each other and as Heart Center types (see pages 74–75) they share certain personality traits. Both have active, "doing" energy, and both are oriented toward accomplishment and helping. They are exuberant, practical, and approval-seeking and often alter themselves to fit whatever image is required. **What distinguishes these two types is that Givers habitually focus on relationships and on others' feelings and needs, in contrast to Performers, who push aside feelings and habitually focus on tasks and goals and getting recognition for their accomplishments.**

S **Types Two and Four.** Givers and Romantics have some personality traits in common because the Giver is the stress type of the Romantic and the Romantic is the security type of the Giver and both are Heart Center types (see pages 74–75). Both are attuned to feelings. Both are sensitive, relationship-oriented, helpful, and emotionally intense. Both have a romantic flare and are concerned with image. Givers feeling secure become more internalized, self-oriented, nostalgic, and uniquely creative. Romantics in stress become more pleasing, outer-directed, focused on others, and giving. **They differ in that Givers are more outer-directed and other-referencing. Givers focus on others' needs with active energy and alter themselves as necessary to meet those needs. In contrast, Romantics are more inner-directed, self-referencing, and subject to feeling "down." Romantics focus on their own specialness or authenticity and are subject to experiencing feelings of deficiency.**

L **Types Two and Five.** Givers and Observers can be considered look-alike types because both types are sensitive to the claims and needs of important others, are quite giving, and do not attend to their own feelings. **However, for Observers the periods of giving and responding to claims made by others are intermittent and punctuated by distinct periods when they move away and disconnect in order to recharge and protect their personal boundaries. Givers, on the other hand, sustain the giving mode, mostly moving forward to connect with others in order to meet others' needs and often lose their personal boundaries in the process.**

L **Types Two and Six.** Givers and Loyal Skeptics can be considered look-alikes because both types can be warm and friendly, anxious, sensitive to others, deferring to what others want or need, and disarming or seductive. (This is especially true of the more phobic, or accommodating, Six.) **However, Givers move forward with active energy, focusing on the needs of important others and often feeling indispensable, while Loyal Skeptics warily hold something back, doubt or question themselves and others, and spurn indispensability. Loyal Skeptics will please others to gain certainty and security rather than to gain love and a sense of self-worth. In contrast, Givers' self-identity is invested in giving.**

L **Types Two and Seven.** Givers and Epicures can be considered look-alike types because both types are active, upbeat, energetic, charming and seductive, friendly, selective in relationships, and eager to be liked. **They differ in that Epicures maintain their separateness, and stay oriented primarily to themselves and to what they like, want, and need, while Givers move toward others and stay oriented primarily to the likes, wants, and needs of others. Epicures can easily get absorbed in their own intellectual pursuits, in contrast to Givers, who alter themselves to meet the emotional needs of others.**

S **Types Two and Eight.** Givers and Protectors share some of the same traits because the Giver is the security type of the Protector and the Protector is the stress type of the Giver. Both show active energy, assertiveness, intrusiveness, generosity, protectiveness toward others, and attraction to power. Givers in stress become more direct and forceful, readily expressing anger and determination that they know what is needed. Protectors feeling secure can be openhearted, expressing feelings, softness, and sensitivity to others. **However, Givers employ their active energy to move toward others with a strong sensitivity to others' feelings and needs, altering themselves to please others and repressing their own needs. By contrast, Protectors use their big energy to act forcefully in a way that often challenges and intimidates others, all the while asserting their own position, sense of justice, wants, and needs.**

L **Types Two and Nine.** Givers and Mediators can be considered look-alike types because they share the characteristic of pleasing others and meeting others' wants and needs. In the process, both orient toward the claims made on them by others and lose awareness of their own needs and priorities. **The main difference is that Givers more *actively* focus their attention and energy on what others need and alter themselves to meet those needs, while Mediators are more *reactive*, allowing themselves to be pulled by whatever claims are made on them. Mediators blend in and disperse their energy to make things comfortable without changing their image. Givers can be intrusive, giving too much; in contrast, Mediators are not intrusive in their giving.**

W **Types Three and Four.** Performers and Romantics look alike because as wings of each other and as Heart Center types (see pages 74–75) they share some personality traits in common. Both have a concern for approval and recognition, and both feel it is important to maintain their image. Both are intense and competitive and have a creative, inventive orientation. **They differ in that Performers sustain a go-ahead goal orientation, which requires them to suspend their feelings, focus attention outward, and alter themselves, while Romantics have difficulty sustaining a goal orientation because of their fluctuating and deep feelings brought on by their preoccupation with relationships and inward focus of attention.**

L **Types Three and Five.** Performers and Observers can be considered look-alike types because both can be oriented toward tasks, objectivity, competency, activities, and getting things done, and at the same time both detach from their feelings or suspend their feelings so as not to be overly influenced by them. **However, Observers are highly mental and are active and energetic in bursts interspersed with distinct periods of retraction—time spent recharging and thinking things over. For Performers, activity is much more continuous. Performers will "keep on trucking" with go-ahead energy and concern about presenting a good image.**

S **Types Three and Six.** Performers and Loyal Skeptics share some of the same personality traits because the Performer is the stress type of the Loyal Skeptic and the Loyal Skeptic is the security type of the Performer. Both types are personable, practical, highly active, and hardworking. Performers feeling secure are more questioning, reflective, and trusting in others to get things done. Loyal Skeptics in stress move into action, get concerned with their image, and press to get goals accomplished. **They differ in that Loyal Skeptics need to get mobilized for action, overcoming perceived pitfalls and doubts, while Performers sustain a goal orientation with their active, go-ahead energy. Performers thrive on success, compliments, and recognition, in contrast to Loyal Skeptics, who are uncomfortable with such feedback and tend to doubt it.**

I **Types Three and Seven.** Performers and Epicures can be considered look-alike types because both types are active, assertive, upbeat, task- and activity-oriented, and often overbooked. Both tend to avoid "negative" feelings such as sadness and sorrow. **They differ in that Epicures naturally focus on their own pleasures and interests and experience a sense of personal entitlement, especially a right to keep their options open, whereas Performers are driven to succeed because they need to maintain their good image and get external approval for what they accomplish in order to sustain their self-worth. Performers strive for efficiency, while Epicures tend not to be interested in efficiency.**

I **Types Three and Eight.** Performers and Protectors can be considered look-alike types because both are assertive, determined, action- and goal-oriented, and willing to take charge. Both types can radiate competence and confidence and may inadvertently step on anyone who gets in their way. **However, Performers shift gears, alter themselves, or change direction, somewhat like chameleons, in order to get their goals accomplished, while Protectors hold to a position, get confrontational, and express anger directly and easily. Performers' anger mostly comes up when they feel obstructed in getting to a goal.**

S **Types Three and Nine.** Performers and Mediators possess some personality traits in common because the Performer is the security type of the Mediator and the Mediator is the stress type of the Performer. Both types are personable, practical, amiable (wanting to be liked), and competent, and both depend on external support and approval. Performers in stress are more likely to get diverted into secondary tasks and put aside their personal agendas and image. Mediators feeling secure become more singularly focused on their own goals, more efficient, and more image-oriented. **They differ in that Performers are fast-paced, efficient, focused on achieving goals, and impatient when obstacles get in their way. Mediators are slower-paced, accommodate readily to the opinions and claims made on them by others, and substitute others' agendas and goals for their own.**

W **Types Four and Five.** Romantics and Observers look alike because as wings of each other they share some of the same personality traits. Both can be analytical, introspective, internalized, sensitive, and shy (yet appear superior). Depending on how much their wings influence them, some Romantics will appear more detached and some Observers appear more in touch with their feelings. **However, Romantics are the most feeling and emotional type—they want more from others and have difficulty keeping their personal boundaries. In contrast, Observers are the most detached type—they want less, stay more self-contained, and keep clearer personal boundaries.**

L **Types Four and Six.** Romantics and counterphobic Loyal Skeptics can be considered look-alike types because both types tend to be contrary, question situations and magnify them, oppose authority, get reckless, break rules, defy dangers, and have periods of self-doubt. **While Loyal Skeptics don't want to become trapped in feelings or longings, Romantics are attracted to feelings and longings. Romantics get expansive and want to be affected emotionally. Furthermore, Loyal Skeptics look for what might go wrong in order to avert or challenge it, while Romantics look for what is missing that could be fulfilling.**

L **Types Four and Seven.** Romantics and Epicures can be considered look-alike types because they are both intense and idealistic and want life to be adventuresome and highly stimulating. They both approach life by focusing on what they want, think, and feel. **However, Epicures are the most upbeat and pleasure-seeking type and avoid pain and negative feelings whenever possible, while Romantics are just the opposite. They tend to become melancholy, to have deep feelings, and to accept pain as part of life.**

L **Types Four and Eight.** Romantics and Protectors can be considered look-alike types because both show intensity, depth, and directness of expression (even flamboyance), a lot of energy or emotion, a desire for authenticity, and tendencies toward recklessness, impulsivity, and opposition. **Because Romantics go deeply into their own feelings, however, they are often internally focused and can fall into inaction and lose direction, whereas Protectors focus externally, surmount their feelings, and sustain action with considerable energy.**

L **Types Four and Nine.** Romantics and Mediators can be considered look-alike types because they are both relationship-oriented, caring, and empathic. Both can get lost or absorbed in their circumstances, feel deficient, become self-deprecating, and lose their impetus for action. **They differ in that Mediators are oriented toward others and like to blend in and keep life steady in order to feel comfortable and avoid conflict. Romantics, by contrast, are oriented toward themselves, are attached to being special or extraordinary, and readily go to extremes or depths of emotions in order to feel vital and alive.**

W **Types Five and Six.** Observers and Loyal Skeptics look alike because as wings of each other and as Head Center types (see pages 74–75), they share some of the same personality traits. Both can be analytical, reflective, thoughtful, hesitant to take action, and retracted (especially the more phobic or accommodating Six). **They differ in that Observers detach from or dampen their feelings, compartmentalize circumstances, and usually delay their responses, while Loyal Skeptics react immediately to circumstances, often intensely and with either fear or action, and they magnify the danger of the circumstances to which they are reacting. Thus, Observers can detach from circumstances, while Loyal Skeptics have difficulty doing so.**

S **Types Five and Seven.** Observers and Epicures share some personality traits because the Observer is the security type of the Epicure and the Epicure is the stress type of the Observer and both are Head Center types (see pages 74–75). Both are self-reliant, knowledgeable, and inventive, and both love ideas. These two types avoid painful feelings. Observers in stress become more externalized, social, active, and oriented toward possibilities. Epicures feeling secure become more internalized, solitary, observant, and inwardly oriented. **They differ in that Observers avoid strong feelings, contain their desires and needs, simplify life, and retract to protect their boundaries. Epicures, on the other hand, actively seek positives, express their desires and needs, get expansive and overbooked, and spurn boundaries and limits.**

S **Types Five and Eight.** Observers and Protectors share some of the same personality traits because the Observer is the stress type of the Protector and the Protector is the security type of the Observer. Both types value respect and truth, resist control, become possessive of space and key resources, and are curious. Observers feeling secure become more engaged and outgoing and express their desires, their feelings, and their anger and position. Protectors in stress become more withdrawn, restrained, and reflective. **However, in general, Observers are the most retracted, contained, and measured type on the Enneagram: they conserve their energy, reduce their needs, and almost always think before acting. Protectors, by contrast, are the most expansive, expressive, and excessive type on the Enneagram: they expand their energy, directly express their desires and their anger, and often act before thinking.**

L **Types Five and Nine.** Observers and Mediators are considered look-alike types because both types can be retracted and introverted, thoughtful and unobtrusive and may even seem to be invisible. Both can pull back from being overly influenced by their surroundings. **They differ in that Observers habitually detach from others and assert their boundaries in self-protection, whereas Mediators are the least able to detach from others; they habitually blend with others and go along with others to keep life harmonious and comfortable.**

W **Types Six and Seven.** Loyal Skeptics and Epicures look alike because as wings of each other and as Head Center types (see pages 74–75) they share some of the same personality traits. Both are mentally quick and often sharp-witted, analytical, imaginative, and able to connect diverse ideas. **Loyal Skeptics put a negative spin on experiences, however, seeing worst-case possibilities and pitfalls, while Epicures put a positive spin on experiences, planning for multiple positive possibilities. Loyal Skeptics welcome reassuring limits and seek to gain certainty. Epicures abhor limits and seek to expand their options. For Loyal Skeptics, pleasure and personal wants are secondary concerns, but for Epicures they are primary.**

L **Types Six and Eight**. Counterphobic Loyal Skeptics and Protectors can be considered look-alike types because both can be aggressive, challenging, and confrontational. Both can seem fearless, and both fight for causes. Both share a view of the world as unfriendly and untrustworthy. **Differences arise, however, in how the two types take action. Loyal Skeptics usually have moments of fear or hesitation before taking action; they may magnify and experience the hazards, and sometimes they give way under pressure as doubts and questions arise. By contrast, Protectors react from instinct; they take action without hesitation, minimize or deny dangers, and hold their ground while denying their vulnerability. Sixes seek certainty, whereas Eights always have it—as the saying goes, they are "often wrong but never in doubt."**

S **Types Six and Nine**. Loyal Skeptics and Mediators have some personality traits in common because the Loyal Skeptic is the stress type of the Mediator and the Mediator is the security type of the Loyal Skeptic. Both Mediators and the more phobic Loyal Skeptics can be agreeable, accommodating, friendly, anxious to please, self-effacing, sensitive, and eager to avoid conflict. Loyal Skeptics feeling secure are more at ease, relaxed, and accepting of life as it is. Mediators in stress become fearful, questioning, wary, and mobilized for action. **However, Loyal Skeptics keep some personal distance, staying focused on potential hazards and what could go wrong, while Mediators, the most other-oriented type, often lose themselves in the requests and claims made on them by others. Mediators go along with others before testing and questioning, whereas Loyal Skeptics test and question before going along with others. Loyal Skeptics are fast-paced in their thinking and reacting, while Mediators take more time to process their thoughts and hence are slower-paced mentally and in their reactions.**

W **Types Seven and Eight**. Epicures and Protectors look alike because as wings of each other they share certain personality traits. Both are self-assertive, express their wants and desires, believe in their own power and ability, resist limits and controls, and are pleasure-oriented. Both have high energy and little inner restraining force. **Epicures avoid pain, explain away or rationalize difficulties, escape conflicts, and go into future planning. Protectors, however, accept pain, engage in difficulties, confront conflicts directly, and live mostly in the present.**

L **Types Seven and Nine**. Epicures and Mediators can be considered look-alike types because both want life to be pleasant and upbeat. They are adaptable and want to be liked and to get along with others. They both avoid conflict. **However, Epicures are more frenetic and fast-paced, while Mediators are more even-tempered and slower-paced. Epicures definitely are oriented toward themselves, knowing and expressing their own wants, agendas, and opinions. In contrast, Mediators are oriented toward others, forgetting or deferring their own wants, agendas, and opinions.**

W **Types Eight and Nine**. Protectors and Mediators look alike because as wings of each other and as Body Center types (see pages 74–75) they share some personality traits. Both enjoy earthy pleasures, have gut reactions, seek comfort, and are friendly and steadfast. Both can get diverted from essential priorities. **The key differences are that Protectors welcome conflict and even anger, while Mediators avoid conflict and anger. Protectors focus on their own opinions, often expressing and defending their opinions as fact. They are decisive. By contrast, Mediators are oriented toward the opinions and views of others and can lose their own positions in deferring to others. They are often indecisive and go along with others to get along.**

How to Confirm and Verify Your Type
Confirming Your Type for Yourself

When you have reached a preliminary decision about the personality type that fits you, consider using the following questions to confirm your decision:

1. When I am under stress or when I mobilize for action, do I shift into some aspects of the stress type connected with the type I believe to be my correct personality type?
2. When I feel relaxed and secure or when I feel *overwhelming* stress, do I shift into some aspects of the security type connected with the type I believe to be my correct personality type?
3. Do I exhibit some of the features of one or both of the wings connected with the type I believe to be my correct personality type?

Verifying Your Type

Once you have discovered and confirmed the personality type that you believe best fits you, consider asking someone who knows you well to objectively verify your personality type. Have that person use the Essential Enneagram Test as well as the Type Description pages to review the personality type you chose and to review the alternative types you considered.

If you would like to learn more about the Enneagram, please see appendix A, "Additional Enneagram Resources."

How to Build Self-Understanding
Value of Self-Observation in Discovering Your Type

Ultimately, you discover your Enneagram personality type and facilitate your personal development by observing how your mind works, what your heart feels, and what your body experiences. To develop self-awareness and self-understanding requires a good self-observer. Self-observation practices are essential to the process of personal, professional, and spiritual development and to the management of personality. Just as physical well-being, fitness, and performance depend on regular exercise, so mental well-being, fitness, and performance depend on practicing regular self-observation.

A fundamental way to develop your ability to observe yourself is to learn and practice the breathing and centering exercise in Section 2 (see pages 72–73). Self-observation practice facilitates not only the development of receptivity and awareness, but ultimately empathy and the ability to reflect in the moment. Self-observation practice also is the basic exercise for noticing where your attention and energy go and what thoughts, feelings, and physical sensations you experience. Through this practice, you can discover your habitual patterns and preoccupations and your embodied core beliefs. Observing these patterns and preoccupations will be very helpful in discovering your Enneagram personality type because they are what distinguish one personality from another. As you develop the skill of observing how you habitually use your attention and energy, you can learn to direct your attention and energy to where you really want them to go. Self-observation skills are fundamental to developing conscious awareness and conscious conduct. Developing these skills can give anyone the ability to see themselves and others more clearly and kindly.

SECTION 2:
What to Do When You Have Discovered Your Type

This section is divided into two parts. All of the information and exercises in the first part apply equally to all nine Enneagram personality types. Part 1 begins with the guidelines for optimal learning followed by a breathing and centering exercise to develop self-observation and receptive awareness. We then describe five general Enneagram principles that will aid you in understanding yourself. Finally, we present the Universal Growth Process (UGP), consisting of the "4As" of awareness, acceptance, action, and adherence.*

Part 2 offers a series of suggested practices that are tailored to each personality type and provides a practical means for pursuing self-development.

PART 1: GENERAL PRACTICES AND PRINCIPLES FOR ALL TYPES

The Guidelines for Optimal Learning

These guidelines apply to any situation, whether pleasant, challenging, or distressing. They are universal. Keep them in mind as you do the practices in this section.

- Let yourself be as centered and grounded in the present moment as you can. The breathing and centering practice that follows provides a how to.
- Allow yourself to have an open, receptive, compassionate heart, beginning with yourself.
- Allow yourself to have an open, receptive, and non-judging mind that is not busy forming responses and defenses.

---

* The Universal Growth Process was cocreated with my teaching associate, Terry Saracino, MA, MBA.

- Let yourself be curious and exploratory, as a child naturally is.
- Anticipate personal gain or value regardless of the difficulty.
- Be committed to making the necessary effort to learn, since all learning requires effort.

Breathing and Centering Steps: Building Receptive Awareness

The following breathing and centering practice is referred to throughout the rest of this section. It is a key tool that can help you as you undertake the suggested practices for personal and professional development. The benefits of this kind of mindfulness practice can be far-reaching both mentally and physically since it helps you develop more flexibility, adaptability, and understanding, as well as the vital skill of reflection, and takes only a few minutes in your day.

This practice is designed to direct your attention inward, to quiet your mind, and to focus your attention. If you wish, you can tape the steps outlined here and then listen to them as you practice. You can practice these steps for a few minutes or for as long as you like. In the beginning, ten to twenty minutes of regular daily practice is optimal. Of course, you can do a breathing practice whenever you feel a need to observe your reactivity and defensiveness, reduce your desire to act on it, and recenter yourself. When you use the breathing exercise for the practices described later in this section, we suggest that you do it for just long enough to recenter yourself.

Steps to Take

1. Sit in a chair comfortably upright with your legs uncrossed and your feet flat on the floor. Close your eyes or soften your gaze to help remove your attention from your external surroundings.
2. Put your attention on your breath, concentrating on it as you breathe in and out. Let your mental state be receptive. Follow your breath, letting your body relax as you breathe. Your breath is a good internal reference point because it is always there in every moment. And your breath provides a neutral focus because it has no content or agenda of its own.
3. As you follow your breath in and down, let it deepen until it seems to disappear right into the gravitational center of your body in the lower abdomen. In this place of grounding deep inside, you have a solid base from which to open your heart and be receptive to yourself and others.

4. When your attention shifts away from your breathing to some thought, feeling, or sensation, just notice it happening. Then let your attention return to your breath. As you continue to follow your breath, you can observe the pattern of your preoccupations and reactions, and through awareness and reflection, gradually become free of them.

5. When you have completed this practice, bring your attention slowly and gently back to your external surroundings. Become aware of yourself sitting in the chair, hear the sounds around you, and open your eyes.

Five General Principles

In this section, we discuss five general principles related to the Enneagram. Each of these five principles has three interrelated components. In learning the principles, it may help you to remember that each principle has three parts. Coming to a deep understanding of these five principles can be very empowering to you as you pursue your personal and professional development.

After reading about each principle, take a few minutes to consider the ways in which you could use that principle in your life. Then do the daily practices associated with that principle.

Principle I: Three Laws of Behavior

1. Wherever your pattern of attention and energy go, your behavior follows.

2. To change your behavior requires self-observation of your pattern of attention and energy.

3. Although self-observation becomes easier as you practice it, it never becomes habitual. Self-observation requires continuing practice.

You can observe for yourself that these three laws of behavior are correct. These laws are central to your development and fundamental to giving both your personal, spiritual, and work lives more meaning and fulfillment. The limiting nature of unmanaged habitual personality reactions often leads to conflict, suffering, and even failure in your personal and professional relationships.

Practice Using the Three Laws of Behavior

On the days you do this practice, take a few minutes at the end of the day to review the following questions. Record your responses in a journal if you like.

- How did I do today at staying aware of my pattern of attention and energy?
- When I reacted automatically to someone or something, was I able to bring back my awareness and redirect my attention and energy?
- How can I better manage my pattern of attention and energy tomorrow?

Principle II: Three Centers of Intelligence

In Western psychology and education, the mind or head has been elevated to prominence as "the" center of intelligence. Yet there is also an intelligence of the heart (emotional intelligence) and an intelligence of the body (sensations and instincts). All three of these intelligences—mind, heart, and body—require ongoing cultivation. Recognizing, developing, and valuing all three centers of intelligence are crucial to all of us in reaching a fulfilling life.

In the Enneagram, the inner triangle of types—Three, Six, and Nine—are the core types of these three centers of intelligence. Each core type has two adjacent types, or wings, that represent variations on the respective core type. Each core type and its two wings constitute a triad. While all types rely on all three centers of intelligence, each of the types relies more heavily on one of the centers—the heart, the mind, or the body, depending on which triad the type is in. This means, for example, that if your type is in the mental or head triad (Five, Six, Seven), you rely more on the Head Center of intelligence to guide you than on the Heart Center of intelligence or the Body Center of intelligence. These centers also represent the three basic needs that we all have for **love** (Heart Center), **security** (Head Center), and **worth** (Body Center) and their corresponding three basic emotions found in all mammals of **distress**, **fear**, and **anger** that occur respectively when **love**, **security**, and/or **worth** are *not met.*

1. *Heart Center.* If you are a Heart Center type—Two, Three, or Four—you tend to perceive the world through the filter of emotional intelligence. You stay attuned to the mood and feeling state in others in order to maintain your feeling of connection with them. You depend more than other types on the approval and recognition of others to support your self-esteem and your desire for love and connection. To ensure that you get that approval and recognition, you create an image of yourself that gets others to accept you and see you as special. All the types depend on emotional intelligence to develop the higher qualities of the Heart Center, such as empathy, understanding, compassion, and loving-kindness. Heart Center types, however, focus more on the need for **love**, connection, affection, bonding, image, and approval. When threatened, distress, panic, and sadness occur.

2. *Head Center.* If you are a Head Center type—Five, Six, or Seven—you tend to filter the world through the mental faculties. The goals of this strategy are to minimize anxiety, to manage potentially painful situations, and to gain a sense of certainty through the mental processes of analyzing, envisioning, imagining, and planning. All the types depend on mental intelligence to develop the higher qualities of the Head Center, such as wisdom, knowing, visioning, and thoughtfulness. But Head Center types focus more on the need for **security**, safety, certainty, assurance, predictability, and opportunity. When threatened, fear and anxiety occur.

3. *Body Center.* If you are a Body Center type—Eight, Nine, or One—you tend to filter the world through an intelligence of kinesthetic and physical sensations and gut instinct. You use personal position and power to make life be the way you sense it should be. You devise strategies that ensure your place in the world and minimize discomfort. All the types depend on the Body Center of intelligence to be in touch with the energy needed for action, to discern how much power to use in situations, and to supply a sense of being grounded in the world. Body Center types, however, focus more on the need for **worth**, congruence, comfort, harmony, belonging, and respect. When threatened, anger and rage occur.

Practice Using the Three Centers of Intelligence

On the days you do this practice, take a few minutes at the end of the day to reflect on the following questions. Record your responses in a journal if you like.

- Given my lead center of intelligence, how did I cultivate all three centers of intelligence today?
- In what ways did I manifest the higher qualities of each center of intelligence today?
- Based on my reflection, what higher qualities do I need to cultivate tomorrow?

Principle III: Three Life Forces

Knowingly or unknowingly, we all operate from three life forces all the time, and all of them are inherent within us.

1. *Active Force.* The active force that provides the energy for action and expression also animates your thoughts, feelings, and imagination. All that you do and accomplish in the material world uses the active force. Sometimes the active force is referred to as the creative, affirming, or positive force, because it makes things happen. Western cultures especially value this force.

2. *Receptive Force.* The receptive force takes in, processes, and digests all the stimuli received by your senses. It is vital to understanding and appreciating the world you live in, to communicating effectively, and to taking right action. Receptivity is the basis of empathy and compassion. It is sometimes referred to as the understanding or negative force, because it takes in and "digests" impressions and because it counters or reacts to active force. Western cultures tend to subordinate the receptive force to the active force and even to devalue it.

3. *Reconciling Force.* The reconciling force is the force of consciousness or awareness. It brings your active and receptive forces into correct proportion—into balance and harmony. In this sense, the reconciling force is the master force that you need to develop in order to carry out right action. The reconciling force is sometimes referred to as the preserving, neutralizing, or neutral force, because it has no position per se but balances the other two forces and ultimately sustains you.

The Serenity Prayer expresses the central role of these three life forces:

God grant me the serenity to accept the things I cannot change (receptive force), the courage to change the things I can (active force), and the wisdom to know the difference (reconciling force).

Mastering these three forces requires recognizing them and understanding how they interact. You need to use your continuing effort every day to bring the active force and the receptive force into awareness and balance.

Practice Balancing the Three Life Forces

On the days you do this practice, take a minute or two at the beginning of the day to become quiet and centered by doing the breathing practice for a short time. Then repeat to yourself one of these two statements:

Today I will practice being receptive to the communications of others and aware of my own inner experience as a guide to my actions.

Today I will practice being aware of my active force and my receptive force and work at balancing them.

Periodically throughout the day, reflect on the statement you chose to repeat to yourself. We suggest that you alternate between these two statements from day to day. Journal your responses to this practice if you like.

Principle IV: Three Survival Behaviors—The Instinctual Subtypes

Human evolution requires three basic survival behaviors, referred to in the Enneagram as the instinctual subtypes: the self-preservation subtype, the social or group subtype, and the one-to-one or intimate subtype. Because these are survival behaviors, each Enneagram personality type includes all three instinctual subtypes. Although you manifest all three to some degree, you usually express one of these three instinctual subtypes more than the other two. Both environmental circumstances and your personality's type structure influence their expression, especially the core emotion associated with your adaptive strategy and what you put your energy into.

1. *Self-Preservation Instinctual Subtype.* Your attention and energy go to issues related to personal survival, such as safety, security, comfort, protection, and adequate basic resources of food, shelter, and warmth.
2. *Social Instinctual Subtype.* Your attention and energy go to issues related to your community and group membership, such as role, status, social acceptance, belonging, participation, and fellowship.
3. *One-to-One Instinctual Subtype.* Your attention and energy go to issues related to connection in vital relationships, such as bonding with special others, sexual intimacy, attractiveness, closeness, union, and merging.

Since these survival instincts are deeply rooted in evolution, it is important to become aware of them operating in your life and how they often drive, even dominate, your behavior. One goal of this awareness is to balance your own instinctual subtype preoccupations appropriately so that no subtype dominates your life. Another goal of this awareness is to be able to accept differences between yourself and others. Without an awareness of the influence of these instinctual subtype preoccupations, you can experience an imbalance in what your energy is devoted to, and you can experience misunderstandings and conflict with others whose preoccupation differs from yours.

Practice Developing Subtype Awareness

On the days you do this practice, set aside a few minutes to reflect on the following questions about subtype behaviors. Remember that all three instinctual subtype behaviors are present in our lives. Journal your responses if you like.

- How do the self-preservation, social, and one-to-one instinctual subtypes manifest themselves in my life, and which one tends to predominate?
- How does my more prominant instinctual subtype preoccupation cause difficulty in my relationships, and how does it benefit them?

- What do I need to do, or stop doing, to bring balance into my life with respect to the instinctual subtypes?

Principle V: Three Levels of Knowing and Learning

We all have three interrelated ways of knowing and learning, and it is useful to be able to distinguish among them. Although the higher levels are more advanced and require more skill, each way has value.

1. *Knowing Based on Your Habit of Mind: Incremental Learning.* This level of knowing and learning is based on your personality type and is determined largely by the core beliefs and attentional style of your type. This level of learning occurs almost automatically through the five senses. It requires little personal awareness because it is based on the habitual thoughts, feelings, and sensations of your type. Once you have identified your personality type, you can use a number of different strategies to promote your personal growth. See the Personal Development section of the Type Description pages for a list of these strategies.

2. *Knowing Based on Conscious Awareness: Reconstructive Learning.* This level of knowing and learning requires that you consciously observe your thoughts, feelings, and sensations. Maintaining awareness of the biases generated by your type's core beliefs, adaptive strategy, and attentional style gives you choice. This level of knowing involves questioning and reflecting on your usual assumptions and replacing your automatic reactions with conscious and deliberate choices. To work at this level of knowing and learning, you need to internalize the material on the Type Description pages and the practices that appear in this section.

3. *Direct Knowing: Transformational Learning.* The third level of knowing and learning harnesses the specific energy of your type and uses it as a transforming agent to transcend your type and its core beliefs, adaptive strategy, and attentional style. Direct knowing is based on a level of awareness that allows even action to precede, not follow, the usual thoughts, feelings, and sensations of your type. Direct knowing, or transformational learning, requires that you be willing to experience your life from a perspective that is not based on a fixed position or identity. It requires that you take an openly receptive stance from which

personality biases can drop away. From this stance, your intellectual curiosity and emotional openness enable you to experience life directly without the distortion or bias of your type. The Enneagram provides you with specific ways to pursue this work of transformation. To master this level of knowing and learning is a lifelong endeavor and entirely voluntary. "The ultimate goal of my development" in the Type Description pages and the reflection practices in this section provide an overview of the transformation tasks.

Elements of Personal, Professional, and Spiritual Development: The Universal Growth Process

The Universal Growth Process (UGP) is a practical and powerful model for personal development that interweaves four components or processes—**awareness, acceptance, action,** and **adherence**. All of these "4As" are required for effective and lasting change. Moreover, they are always present to some extent, and they are simple to learn and recall, which further increases their value.

Awareness

Use the breathing and centering practice described earlier or your own practice to increase your receptivity and grounded presence. This is fundamental to self-observing your adaptive strategy, with its interwoven pattern of attention and energy; to working with your stress and anger (your reactivity); to grasping and releasing from no longer valid core beliefs; and to heightening your flexibility, adaptability, and understanding. Change, growth, and development depend on awareness. And the practice provides a basis for reflection "on the spot" when you are faced with challenges, distress, or reactivity.

Acceptance

Open your heart to yourself and others to accept whatever arises in the moment. This means manifesting compassion by adopting a kind and caring attitude toward yourself and others. Acceptance includes befriending your reactivity and working with judgments of self and others and with the associated feelings and sensations. Acceptance does not mean agreeing or condoning.

Remember that you can work only from where you are, since everyone is in a different place in his or her journey.

Action

Action involves three inter-related steps.

1. *Pause.*

   Notice your reactions, upsets, and distress and then *pause,* by breathing and centering, to *collect* your energy back into yourself—into the gravitational center of your body in the belly—so as to *contain* it when it wants to discharge into old habitual reactions and behaviors. Briefly put: Notice → pause → collect energy → contain.

2. *Inquiry.*

   Next practice thoughtful and gentle reflection and inquiry in order to discover, *discern,* and work with whatever reactivity—such as upset, anger, or distress—or theme, especially type sturcture, that arises in the moment. *This is where the Enneagram understandings provide ultimate value.* Adopt a stance of genuine curiosity to know the truth. Inquiry involves considering what your usual reactivity and automatic responses are about. These responses are keys to development and change because they mainly involve:

   - Our key identifications, our core beliefs, and the associated concerns and feelings deeply embedded in our type structure
   - Our personal stories and wounds

3. *Conscious Conduct.*

   Let your "inner coach" be your mentor by gently encouraging you into conscious conduct, which manifests in two interrelated forms:

   - *Releasing into acceptance* by staying with the experience or felt sense of → loosening → letting go → and reexperiencing the fundamental principle you lost sight of (see Practice Reflecting for each type in Specific Practice section that follows). Remember that the higher qualities in the ultimate goal of your development don't come and go—your being in touch with them comes and goes.
   - *Taking action* by staying with the experience or felt sense → of loosening → and moving into compassionate action respectful of self and other.

Adherence

Adherence simply means commitment to the process of the "4As" and to daily practice. We all have many opportunities each day to recommit as we go on automatic and get reactive. Motivation for adherence carries with it expectation of benefit and ultimately a hope for greater happiness. Thus, intention is an irreducible ingredient. Adherence honors the principle that new learning is a combination of observation, experience, and practice, for we all have minds and bodies characterized by neuroplasticity—the ability to form new neural pathways. Through adherence you can internalize the Universal Growth Process of the "4 As" and carry out regular assessment of your growth.

PART 2: SPECIFIC PRACTICES FOR EACH TYPE

For each of the nine personality types, you will find five specific practices:

Practice receptive awareness. This practice builds your self-observer and focuses on a key aspect of your type.

Practice taking action. This practice focuses on changing a habitual behavior associated with your type.

Practice previewing and reviewing your progress. This practice gives you the opportunity to work on the central issue of your type. This is a key practice for development.

Practice the "4As" of awareness, acceptance, action, and adherence. This practice builds up your acceptance and personal mastery by helping you befriend your reactivity, anger, and defensiveness and develop conscious conduct through both letting go and taking compassionate and respectful action. See the preceeding section on the Universal Growth Process on page 80 for a detailed description.

Practice reflecting to reclaim your higher qualities. This practice leads you to reclaim the fundamental principle associated with your type and to pursue the ultimate task of self-development for your type.

Practices for the Perfectionist (Type One)

We recommend that you begin by choosing just one practice to work on before you move on to the others. It may take you a week or so with each practice to experience a sense of progress. You might find it helpful to keep a journal to record your daily responses to these practices. And you may want to record these practices so that you can listen to them as helpful reminders.

Practice Receptive Awareness

Pay particular attention to your inner critic and its incessant demands. Stop several times a day for a minute or so to reflect by breathing down and in, allowing yourself to become aware and receptive. Then consider the following questions:

How have I been judging myself and others? How constantly present has the voice of judgment been? How has my inner critic made me feel? What bodily sensations go with judgments? In what ways has my inner critic been affecting my behavior?

Practice Taking Action

Recall that Perfectionists tend to be dominated by the demands of their inner critic to always do what is correct and responsible. Consequently, they end up suppressing their personal needs and their natural desires for pleasure. Here is a practice:

Each day, I will consciously and deliberately include time for personal needs, natural desires, and pleasurable activities (at least some of which have nothing to do with self-improvement per se) and I will schedule inviolate time for these activities.

I will do my best to notice when internal resistance to doing enjoyable things comes up and use this resistance as a signal to go ahead and do them.

To check your progress, notice if you are experiencing a better balance of work and pleasure in your life. Remember that Perfectionists can get so driven by their sense of responsibility and their drive to do work before pleasure that they never get to the pleasure.

Practice Previewing and Reviewing Your Progress

Preview:

When you first get up in the morning, center yourself by practicing the breathing exercise for a few moments. Then say to yourself:

Today I will practice accepting my own and others' mistakes and errors as part of the natural flow of life. I will practice appreciating different points of view, different values, and different ways of doing things. I can do this by noticing and releasing resentments when they arise, hence practicing forgiveness. I will try to bring a sense of harmony and balance between work and pleasure into my life today.

When you do this practice, adopt the stance that the changes you are previewing are already true about you, since what you came to believe and the associated adaptive strategy basically are no longer true.

Review:

In the evening each day, take a few minutes to review your progress. Ask yourself, with an open mind and heart:

How did I do today at accepting mistakes and errors? At appreciating differences? At forgiving? At experiencing a sense of harmony and balance between work and pleasure? Did I get caught up in feeling resentful about others' mistakes and errors?

Use what you learn from this review to guide your thoughts and actions for the next day's preview and review practice.

Practice the "4As" of Awareness, Acceptance, Action, and Adherence

You can do this practice a number of times each day, theoretically as often as you notice your reactivity. Note that the "4As" process is clearly embedded in this practice. It may help in doing this practice to use "I" instead of "you" statements. In committing to this practice, you virtually make life your mindfulness practice. Here is the practice:

When you get upset or reactive, *notice* that the source of your distress is unfairness, irresponsibility, or something that cannot be corrected, fueled by your tension and suppressed anger and resentment.

Pause to *collect* back and *contain* the energy of your reactivity by breathing down into your belly.

Through *non-judgmental inquiry,* can you become aware that your reactivity comes from your core belief that you must be right, good, and responsible to be worthy and that you must avoid being so wrong and bad that you end up unworthy?

With *discernment* can you realize that this belief most likely is just an old habit of mind and gently coach yourself into *letting go* and appreciating differences and accepting life as it is?

Can you also gently coach yourself into *action* that is respectful to yourself and others and integrates pleasure with healthy restraint?

Remind yourself to notice and absorb how acceptance of self and others is received and welcomed.

Practice Reflecting to Reclaim Your Higher Qualities

At least once a week, take a few minutes in a quiet place to reflect upon and contemplate both the fundamental principle and the ultimate task for Perfectionists. A natural outdoor setting is an ideal place to do this. Simply reflect on the following:

> *The* fundamental principle *that Perfectionists lose sight of and need to reclaim is that we are all one and we are perfect as we are. Therefore, the* ultimate task *for Perfectionists is to reclaim perfection by regaining a sense that life is as it is, not divided into right and wrong as Perfectionists perceive it to be. This ultimate task is more easily accomplished when you accept differences and mistakes, experience compassion and forgiveness toward yourself and others, and allow yourself time to relax and enjoy life.*

Then explore what adopting these truths would mean to your life. You are likely to experience increasing acceptance of life as it is—the inner peacefulness and serenity that naturally result from this practice.

Practices for the Giver (Type Two)

We recommend that you begin by choosing just one practice to work on before you move on to the others. It may take you a week or more with each practice to experience a sense of progress. You might find it helpful to keep a journal to record your daily responses to these practices. And you may want to record these practices so that you can listen to them as helpful reminders.

Practice Receptive Awareness

Pay particular attention to how much your attention and energy go to the needs and feelings of others. Stop several times a day for a minute or so to reflect by breathing down and in, allowing yourself to become aware and receptive. Then consider the following questions:

How much of my attention and energy have gone into responding to others' wants, needs, and feelings? What have I done when I've seen that someone or something needs my help? In what ways have I been adapting myself to meet others' expectations? What happens inside me when I don't feel appreciated?

Practice Taking Action

Recall that Givers tend to believe they must fulfill others' needs in order to gain approval and love. Here is a practice:

Each day I will make a conscious effort to ask myself what I want and need from both myself and others, and deliberately make my own wants and needs a priority.
I will do my best to notice that when a feeling of selfishness or guilt comes up it can stop me from taking care of myself or from asking what I need from others. If I notice a rising emotional intensity in myself, I will use this feeling as a clue that I am not paying sufficient attention to my own wants and needs.

To check your progress, notice if you are really feeling nurtured. Remember that Givers have a powerful tendency to repress their own needs and become absorbed in fulfilling others' needs.

Practice Previewing and Reviewing Your Progress

Preview:

When you first get up in the morning, center yourself by practicing the breathing exercise for a few moments. Then say to yourself:

Today I will practice giving and receiving equally as my own needs and others' needs become apparent to me. I will practice doing this with an open and generous heart. I can do this by taking time to develop my own independence and autonomy, by nurturing my own interests, and by looking out for my own well-being as conscientiously as I look out for the interests and well-being of others.

When you do this practice, adopt the stance that the changes you are previewing are already true about you, since what you came to believe and the associated adaptive strategy basically are no longer true.

Review:

In the evening each day, take a few minutes to review your progress. Ask yourself, with an open mind and heart:

How did I do today in giving and receiving equally? How did I do in being open and generous toward myself as well as others? Did I take time to fulfill my own interests and needs? What did I allow myself to receive from others? Did I get caught up in feeling prideful or indispensable?

Use what you learn from this review to guide your thoughts and actions for the next day's preview and review practice.

Working with the "4As" of Awareness, Acceptance, Action, and Adherence

You can do this practice a number of times each day, theoretically as often as you notice your reactivity. Note that the "4As" process is clearly embedded in this practice. It may help in doing this practice to use "I" instead of "you" statements. In committing to this practice, you virtually make life your mindfulness practice. Here is the practice:

When you get upset or reactive *notice* that you are feeling frustrated in your desire to help and in your conviction that you know best what is needed in the situation, fueled by a feeling of pride and a sense of indispensability.

Pause to *collect* back and *contain* the energy of your reactivity by breathing down into your belly.

Through *non-judgmental inquiry,* can you become aware that your reactivity comes from your core belief that you must fulfill the needs of others in order to be loved and approved and to avoid feeling useless and hence dispensable?

With *discernment* can you realize that this belief most likely is just an old habit of mind and gently coach yourself into *letting go* of it, realizing that in relationships it is just as good to receive as it is to give?

Can you also gently coach yourself into *action* that is respectful to yourself and others and openheartedly integrates your and others' needs? Then you can engage in what really is needed freely from your own separate self.

Remind yourself to notice and absorb that love naturally flows both from and to you.

Practice Reflecting to Reclaim Your Higher Qualities

At least once a week, take a few minutes in a quiet place to reflect upon and contemplate both the fundamental principle and the ultimate task for Givers. A natural outdoor setting is an ideal place to do this. Simply reflect on the following:

> *The* fundamental principle *that Givers lose sight of and need to reclaim is that everyone's needs can be equally and freely met. Therefore, the* ultimate task *for Givers is to realize that being loved and receiving approval are not dependent on being needed and don't depend on how much you give to others. This ultimate task is more easily accomplished when you realize that paying attention to your own personal wants and needs and receiving what you want and need from others is as important as taking care of the wants and needs of others.*

Then explore what adopting these truths would mean to your life. You are likely to experience an increasing sense of calm, freedom, and humility or humbleness that naturally result from this practice.

Practices for the Performer (Type Three)

We recommend that you begin by choosing just one practice to work on before you move on to the others. It may take you a week or more with each practice to experience a sense of progress. You might find it helpful to keep a journal to record your daily responses to these practices. And you may want to record these practices so that you can listen to them as helpful reminders.

Practice Receptive Awareness

Pay particular attention to your feelings and your tendency to put them aside in favor of efficient action. Stop several times a day for a minute or so to reflect by breathing down and in, allowing yourself to become aware and receptive. Then consider the following questions:

What feelings have occurred in me since I last stopped to check? What tasks was I putting my energy into when these feelings came up? How have I avoided or suspended these feelings? Have I taken any time to slow my pace and "smell the flowers"?

Practice Taking Action

Recall that Performers often suspend or avoid feelings because feelings seem to get in the way of efficient action. Here is a practice:

Each day I will make a conscious effort to moderate my pace at work and in my personal life.
I will do my best to notice my hard-driving energy, my time urgency and impatience, and my preoccupation with things to do. Knowing that my tendency is to do everything fast, I will stop myself for a few moments, and breathe deeply and slowly, allowing my attention to follow my breath into the center of my body and away from the demands of the world. Then, in this quieter state, I will determine to practice a more moderate pace.

To check your progress, notice if you are taking the time to be aware of your own feelings and to really listen to others. Remember that Performers can get so focused on setting multiple goals and achieving results that they screen out their own feelings and what others are trying to communicate to them.

Practice Previewing and Reviewing Your Progress

Preview:

When you first get up in the morning, center yourself by practicing the breathing exercise for a few moments. Then say to yourself:

Today I will practice knowing that getting things done is not solely dependent on my own effort and efficiency. I will practice letting go of constant doing and become more conscious of what I really need to do. I can do this by staying in touch with my feelings and letting them guide me.

When you do this practice, adopt the stance that the changes you are previewing are already true about you, since what you came to believe and the associated adaptive strategy basically are no longer true.

Review:

In the evening each day, take a few minutes to review your progress. Ask yourself, with an open mind and heart:

How did I do today at distinguishing between what I could let go of and what I could accomplish? How receptive was I to my real feelings and to maintaining a pace in harmony with my whole being?

Use what you learn from this review to guide your thoughts and actions for the next day's preview and review practice.

Working with the "4As" of Awareness, Acceptance, Action, and Adherence

You can do this practice a number of times each day, theoretically as often as you notice your reactivity. Note that the "4As" process is clearly embedded in this practice. It may help in doing this practice to use "I" instead of "you" statements. In committing to this practice, you virtually make life your mindfulness practice. Here is the practice:

When you get upset or reactive, *notice* that you are being thwarted in your efforts to accomplish your tasks and goals and to get approval by doing things, and that your frustration is being fueled by your go-ahead energy, which blocks your heartfelt feelings.

Pause to *collect* back and *contain* the energy of your reactivity by breathing down into your belly.

Through *non-judgmental inquiry,* can you become aware that your reactivity comes from your core belief that you gain love and approval primarily through what you do and accomplish and by how well you avoid being incompetent and an utter failure?

With *discernment* can you realize that this belief most likely is just an old habit of mind and gently coach yourself into *letting go,* realizing that love comes from being as well as from doing?

Can you also gently coach yourself into *action* that is respectful to yourself and others and integrates feeling with action? Notice your pace and slow it down; ease up on the pressure you put on yourself. Let your heart be receptive to your own true feelings and to others.

Remind yourself to notice and absorb the reality that love is not dependent on what you accomplish.

Practice Reflecting to Reclaim Your Higher Qualities

At least once a week, take a few minutes in a quiet place to reflect upon and contemplate both the fundamental principle and the ultimate task for Performers. A natural outdoor setting is an ideal place to do this. Simply reflect on the following:

> *The* fundamental principle *that Performers lose sight of and need to reclaim is that everything works and gets done naturally according to universal laws, not simply by the individual efforts of the doer. Therefore, the* ultimate task *for Performers is to know that recognition and love come from who you are, not from what you do. This ultimate task is more easily accomplished when you accept that constant accomplishment is not what life is about.*

Then explore what adopting these truths would mean to your life. This practice is likely to help you experience a moderated pace as well as the veracity of your own true feelings that naturally result from this practice.

Practices for the Romantic (Type Four)

We recommend that you begin by choosing just one practice to work on before you move on to the others. It may take you a week or more with each practice to experience a sense of progress. You might find it helpful to keep a journal to record your daily responses to these practices. And you may want to record these practices so that you can listen to them as helpful reminders.

Practice Receptive Awareness

Pay particular attention to how much time you spend missing and longing for things that feel important but are not present in your life. Stop several times a day for a minute or so to reflect by breathing down and in, allowing yourself to become aware and receptive. Then consider the following questions:

> *What have I been feeling disappointed about? What have I been feeling that there's not enough of in my life? How has what seems special or ideal, but not available, been influencing me? How has my attention been going to what is missing rather than what is present? How have I abandoned my heart, my good feeling about myself? What or who have I been experiencing as just fine and not lacking in any way?*

Practice Taking Action

Recall that Romantics often get so absorbed in what would be ideal but is lacking that they tend to miss what is positive about the present. Here is a practice:

> *Each day I will consciously embrace and appreciate the ordinary experiences of everyday life. I will appreciate the little things, such as necessary daily tasks, ordinary encounters with others, and whatever beauty is around me.*
>
> *When I notice my attention drifting away to what is missing or I begin to feel disappointed with the way things are, I will do my best to use this experience as a signal to return my attention to the present and to make the ordinary meaningful.*

To check your progress, notice if you are experiencing the present as more fulfilling and less disappointing. Remember that Romantics, because their attention is absorbed in past and future ideals, often fail to appreciate much of ordinary everyday life.

Practice Previewing and Reviewing Your Progress

Preview:

When you first get up in the morning, center yourself by practicing the breathing exercise for a few moments. Then say to yourself:

Today I will practice living in emotional balance and sustaining a steady course of action, despite any fluctuating feelings I experience. I can do this by not being swayed by strong emotions or dominated by what is disappointing, and by appreciating what is positive and meaningful in the flow of life.

When you do this practice, adopt the stance that the changes you are previewing are already true about you, since what you came to believe and the associated adaptive strategy basically are no longer true.

Review:

In the evening each day, take a few minutes to review your progress. Ask yourself, with an open mind and heart:

How did I do today at appreciating what is present and fulfilling in my life rather than lamenting what is absent and disappointing? Did I sustain a steady course of action despite fluctuating feelings? Did I resist getting absorbed in strong feelings of longing or envy? Did I experience more of a sense of wholeness?

Use what you learn from this review to guide your thoughts and actions for the next day's preview and review practice.

Working with the "4As" of Awareness, Acceptance, Action, and Adherence

You can do this practice a number of times each day, theoretically as often as you notice your reactivity. Note that the "4As" process is clearly embedded in this practice. It may help in doing this practice to use "I" instead of "you" statements. In committing to this practice, you virtually make life your mindfulness practice. Here is the practice:

When you get upset or reactive *notice* that you are concerned about disappointments and what you feel is missing from your life and that your feelings are fueled by your deep longing and envy for what others seem to have.

Pause to *collect* back and *contain* the energy of your reactivity by breathing down into your belly.

Through *non-judgmental inquiry,* can you become aware that your reactivity comes from your core belief that in order to be truly loved you must obtain the ideal love or situation and avoid the feeling that you are lacking and deficient?

With *discernment* can you realize that this belief most likely is just an old habit of mind and gently coach yourself into *letting go,* realizing that life and love are based on what is present, not what is missing? Notice that your intense emotions come from an inner sense of loss, of lacking. Steady yourself in the present with what is here and now.

Can you also gently coach yourself into *action* that is respectful to yourself and others with a focus on what is present, not what is missing?

Remind yourself to notice and absorb that wholeness exists in what you already are and in your acceptance of others as they are.

Practice Reflecting to Reclaim Your Higher Qualities

At least once a week, take a few minutes in a quiet place to reflect upon and contemplate both the fundamental principle and the ultimate task for Romantics. A natural outdoor setting is an ideal place to do this. Simply reflect on the following:

> *The* fundamental principle *that Romantics lose sight of and need to reclaim is that everyone can have a deep and complete connection to all others and all things. Therefore, the* ultimate task *for Romantics is to realize that a sense of wholeness and love come from appreciating what is already present in the here and now. This ultimate task is more easily accomplished when you realize that feelings of something missing are a consequence of idealizing the past and the future instead of focusing on satisfaction in the present.*

Then explore what adopting these truths would mean to your life. You are likely to experience the sense of gratitude for what is and even equanimity that naturally result from this practice.

Practices for the Observer (Type Five)

We recommend that you begin by choosing just one practice to work on before you move on to the others. It may take you a week or more with each practice to experience a sense of progress. You might find it helpful to keep a journal to record your daily responses to these practices. And you may want to record these practices so that you can listen to them as helpful reminders.

Practice Receptive Awareness

Pay particular attention to your tendency to limit your emotional involvement and connection by detaching from your feelings and disengaging from others. Stop several times a day for a minute or so to reflect by breathing down and in, allowing yourself to become aware and receptive. Then consider the following questions:

> *How have I been limiting my emotional involvement? My engagement with and connection to others? In what ways have I been avoiding my own and others' feelings? When others have expressed their emotions, have I detached and withdrawn into my mind?*

Practice Taking Action

Recall that Observers often detach from their feelings and disengage from others because they are concerned that others might intrude upon them and demand too much of them. Here is a practice:

> *Each day I will make a conscious effort to practice a sense of abundance. I will act from the position that there are ample resources and energy. I will give more of myself and receive more from the world around me.*
>
> *I will do my best to observe and counter my tendency to withdraw to conserve energy, and use this as a signal to stay present and connected.*

To check your progress, notice if you are staying more connected to your feelings and more engaged with others rather than reverting to your inclination to retract or withdraw. Remember that a sense of abundance seems counter-instinctive to Observers, who are concerned about scarcity and the depletion of energy in a world they believe takes too much and gives too little. And allow yourself to realize that retracting actually robs you of energy.

Practice Previewing and Reviewing Your Progress

Preview:

When you first get up in the morning, center yourself by practicing the breathing exercise for a few moments. Then say to yourself:

Today I will practice staying engaged in what is going on around me. I will practice maintaining my connection to others and to my own feelings. I can do this by observing my tendency to withdraw and disconnect and by counteracting this tendency.

When you do this practice, adopt the stance that the changes you are previewing are already true about you, since what you came to believe and the associated adaptive strategy basically are no longer true.

Review:

In the evening each day, take a few minutes to review your progress. Ask yourself, with an open mind and heart:

How did I do today at keeping myself engaged in the flow of life? What did I do to stay connected to others and to my feelings? How did I reverse my self-protective tendency to retract and withdraw?

Use what you learn from this review to guide your thoughts and actions for the next day's preview and review practice.

Working with the "4As" of Awareness, Acceptance, Action, and Adherence

You can do this practice a number of times each day, theoretically as often as you notice your reactivity. Note that the "4As" process is clearly embedded in this practice. It may help in doing this practice to use "I" instead of "you" statements. In committing to this practice, you virtually make life your mindfulness practice. Here is the practice:

When you get upset or reactive, *notice* that your tendency to detach from feelings and protect yourself from intrusion gets fueled by the energy of your withdrawal and by avarice for what you just can't do without is being blocked.

Pause to *collect* back and *contain* the energy of your reactivity by breathing down into your belly.

Through *non-judgmental inquiry,* can you become aware that your reactivity comes from your core belief that you must protect yourself from a world that demands too much and gives too little in order to assure life and security and to avoid being drained of life energy?

With *discernment* can you realize that this belief most likely is just an old habit of mind and gently coach yourself into *letting go,* realizing that the flow of life provides ample energy for you to fully engage in your feelings and affirm life?

Can you also gently coach yourself into *action* that is respectful to yourself and others and provides mutual support and engagement? Let yourself act in congruence with both head and heart.

Remind yourself to notice and absorb how you are fulfilled, not emptied, through this process.

Practice Reflecting to Reclaim Your Higher Qualities

At least once a week, take a few minutes in a quiet place to reflect upon and contemplate both the fundamental principle and the ultimate task for Observers. A natural outdoor setting is an ideal place to do this. Simply refect on the following:

> *The* fundamental principle *that Observers lose sight of and need to reclaim is that there is an ample supply of all the knowledge and energy everyone needs. Therefore, the* ultimate task *for Observers is to stay engaged in the flow of life, supplying and receiving energy freely. This ultimate task is more easily accomplished when you experience the fact that staying connected with your feelings and with others does not deplete you but instead supports you.*

Then explore what adopting these truths would mean to your life. You are likely to experience the freer flow of life energy and sense of engagement and support from others that naturally results from this practice.

Practices for the Loyal Skeptic (Type Six)

We recommend that you begin by choosing just one practice to work on before you move on to the others. It may take you a week or more with each practice to experience a sense of progress. You might find it helpful to keep a journal to record your daily responses to these practices. And you may want to record these practices so that you can listen to them as helpful reminders.

Practice Receptive Awareness

Pay particular attention to how much your attention and energy go to imagining worst-case scenarios and selecting information that supports negative, harmful possibilities. Stop several times a day for a minute or so to reflect by breathing down and in, allowing yourself to become aware and receptive. Then consider the following questions:

What harmful or hazardous outcomes have come to my mind? What has felt threatening to me? Unpredictable? Untrustworthy? How have I been watchful, wary, cautious, or challenging? What self-doubts and worst-case scenarios have been preoccupying me? How have I been dwelling on what could go wrong?

Practice Taking Action

Recall that Loyal Skeptics tend to question, doubt, and fear or challenge what could go wrong because of a loss of trust in themselves and others. Here is the practice:

Each day I will make a conscious effort to take appropriate action despite doubt or fear. I will do my best to face what seem like hazards, not avoid them (a phobic response) or challenge them (a counterphobic response).

When I feel apprehensive, anxious, or fearful (phobic)—or tense, hyper, or challenging (counterphobic)—I will do my best to center and ground myself by breathing deeply and then move forward into action, reminding myself that fear does not have to go away before I go into action.

To check your progress, notice if you are taking appropriate action without having to first dispel fear or excessively test and validate your course of action. Remember that Loyal Skeptics habitually avoid hazards (a phobic response) or challenge them (a counterphobic response). As a way of coping with doubt and fear, phobic Sixes seek security and counterphobic Sixes defy security. Flight and fight are both responses to perceived hazards.

Practice Previewing and Reviewing Your Progress

Preview:

When you first get up in the morning, center yourself by practicing the breathing exercise for a few moments. Then say to yourself:

Today I will practice acting with faith in myself and trust in others, just as a person who already has these qualities would act. I can do this by taking action before I have proof or certainty about my course of action and by believing in my own resources and abilities.

When you do this practice, adopt the stance that the changes you are previewing are already true about you, since what you came to believe and the associated adaptive strategy basically are no longer true.

Review:

In the evening each day, take a few minutes to review your progress. Ask yourself, with an open mind and heart:

How did I do today at having faith in myself and trust in others? In what ways did I move forward into action without having to dispel fear or gain certainty about my course of action? How well did I steady my attention on what is positive?

Use what you learn from this review to guide your thoughts and actions for the next day's preview and review practice.

Practice Working with the "4As" of Awareness, Acceptance, Action, and Adherence

You can do this practice a number of times each day, theoretically as often as you notice your reactivity. Note that the "4As" process is clearly embedded in this practice. It may help in doing this practice to use "I" instead of "you" statements. In committing to this practice, you virtually make life your mindfulness practice. Here is the practice:

When you get upset or reactive, *notice* that you are focused on and magnifying hazards and mistrusting what and whom you can count on, fueled by underlying fear and doubt. If you lean toward the counterphobic, notice your contrary thinking and need to face challenges.

Pause to *collect* back and *contain* the energy of your reactivity by breathing down into your belly.

Through *non-judgmental inquiry,* can you become aware that your reactivity comes from your core belief that you must seek certainty and security in a hazardous and unpredictable world and avoid becoming helpless and dependent in this kind of world?

With *discernment* can you realize that this belief most likely is just an old habit of mind and gently coach yourself into *letting go* of it, realizing that you have lost your faith in yourself and trust in others?

Can you also gently coach yourself into *action* that is respectful to yourself and others and provides trust-based support? Allow the energy in your imaginings, your "negative spin" on life, to be turned into an ability to see the positives.

And from a base of trust, *remind* yourself to notice and absorb that there is no substitute for real faith in yourself and the universe.

Practice Reflecting to Reclaim Your Higher Qualities

At least once a week, take a few minutes in a quiet place to reflect upon and contemplate both the fundamental principle and the ultimate task for Loyal Skeptics. A natural outdoor setting is an ideal place to do this. Simply reflect on the following:

The fundamental principle *that Loyal Skeptics lose sight of and need to regain is that we can all have faith in ourselves, in others, and in the world. Therefore, the* ultimate task *for Loyal Skeptics is to trust self and others. This ultimate task is more easily accomplished when you notice your doubt or fear and calm it, when you move ahead in spite of lingering doubt or fear, when you don't automatically challenge hazards, and when you accept uncertainty as a natural part of life.*

Then explore what adopting these truths would mean to your life. You are likely to experience the inner assurance, calmness, and quieter mind that naturally result from this practice.

Practices for the Epicure (Type Seven)

We recommend that you begin by choosing just one practice to work on before you move on to the others. It may take you a week or more with each practice to experience a sense of progress. You might find it helpful to keep a journal to record your daily responses to these practices. And you may want to record these practices so that you can listen to them as helpful reminders.

Practice Receptive Awareness

Pay particular attention to how much your attention and energy go to planning for pleasurable, positive possibilities. Stop several times a day for a minute or so to reflect by breathing down and in, allowing yourself to become aware and receptive. Then consider the following questions:

How have I been turning my mind to new and interesting activities when faced with something potentially negative? How have I circumvented frustrations? What various options and opportunities have been absorbing my attention and energy? How have I been escaping what might be painful?

Practice Taking Action

Recall that Epicures try to avoid fear, pain, and limitations by generating multiple positive options for themselves. But Epicures actually limit themselves by habitually steering away from anything that could involve distress, fear, or pain. Here is a practice:

Each day I will consciously practice following through on every agreement I make and on all the responsibilities I have undertaken, despite the pains and frustrations I may experience.

I will do my best to recognize my tendency to escape what feels limiting or negative, and notice how I come up with good reasons and alternatives for getting out of what doesn't seem or feel positive. I will do my best to notice when something (like this practice) starts to seem frustrating and limiting to me. I will use that as a signal to "hold my feet to the fire"—to continue what I have started.

To check your progress, notice if you are fulfilling the agreements and responsibilities that you find tedious, frustrating, or unpleasant. Notice too how this feels. Remember that the Epicure strategy of keeping life upbeat and boundless can make you susceptible to the desire to escape from painful or frustrating situations.

Practice Previewing and Reviewing Your Progress

Preview:

When you first get up in the morning, center yourself by practicing the breathing exercise for a few moments. Then say to yourself:

> *Today I will practice keeping my attention and energy in the present moment, no matter what frustrations and painful feelings life presents to me. I will also practice keeping others in mind, and not just my own agenda. I can do this by accepting all of life in the here and now and by staying aware of my tendency to divert my attention and energy into planning for pleasurable options and future opportunities.*

When you do this practice, adopt the stance that the changes you are previewing are already true about you, since what you came to believe and the associated adaptive strategy basically are no longer true.

Review:

In the evening each day, take a few minutes to review your progress. Ask yourself, with an open mind and heart:

> *How did I do today at keeping my attention and energy in the present moment? How did I do at keeping in mind the well-being of others as well as my own well-being? How well did I keep my commitment to doing this practice? In what ways did I allow myself to experience and stay with frustrating and painful experiences?*

Use what you learn from this review to guide your thoughts and actions for the next day's preview and review practice.

Working with the "4As" of Awareness, Acceptance, Action, and Adherence

You can do this practice a number of times each day, theoretically as often as you notice your reactivity. Note that the "4As" process is clearly embedded in this practice. It may help in doing this practice to use "I" instead of "you" statements. In committing to this practice, you virtually make life your mindfulness practice. Here is the practice:

When you get upset or reactive, *notice* that you are experiencing limitations on your freedom and your effort to keep life up and flowing and that your frustration is fueled by gluttony of the mind for positive options, opportunities, and adventures.

Pause to *collect* back and *contain* the energy of your reactivity by breathing down into your belly.

Through *non-judgmental inquiry*, can you become aware that your reactivity comes from your core belief that you must keep life up and open in order to have the good and secure life and avoid or escape being stuck in pain and suffering?

With *discernment* can you realize that this belief most likely is just an old habit of mind and gently coach yourself into *letting go*, realizing that the wholeness of life includes pain and sadness as well as pleasure and joy?

Can you also gently coach yourself into *action* that is respectful to yourself and others and open-heartedly honors all of life?

Deepen your concentration and focus and *remind* yourself to notice and absorb that honoring the full life means embracing all of life, its sorrows as well as its joys, its limits as well as its possibilities.

Practice Reflecting to Reclaim Your Higher Qualities

At least once a week, take a few minutes in a quiet place to reflect upon and contemplate both the fundamental principle and the ultimate task for Epicures. A natural outdoor setting is an ideal place to do this. Simply reflect on the following:

The fundamental principle *that Epicures lose sight of and need to regain is that life is a full spectrum of possibilities to be experienced deeply and with sustained concentration. Therefore, the* ultimate task *for Epicures is to accept that a complete life contains a spectrum of joy and sorrow, pleasure and pain, opportunity and limitation. This ultimate task is more easily accomplished when you accept all of life in the present moment, keep grounded despite uncomfortable emotions or tedious tasks, and stay present to both yourself and others with focused concentration.*

Then explore what adopting these truths would mean to your life. You are likely to experience the greater wholeness, acceptance of all of life, and deeper sense of joy that naturally result from this practice.

Practices for the Protector (Type Eight)

We recommend that you begin by choosing just one practice to work on before you move on to the others. It may take you a week or more with each practice to experience a sense of progress. You might find it helpful to keep a journal to record your daily responses to these practices. And you may want to record these practices so that you can listen to them as helpful reminders.

Practice Awareness

Pay particular attention to both the positive and negative impact of your energy on others. Stop several times a day for a minute or so to reflect by breathing down and in, allowing yourself to become aware and receptive. Then consider the following questions:

> *What has been the impact of my energy and the way I express myself on others? In what ways have I evoked resistance or confrontation? Have I caused others to back off from me or to withdraw into themselves? How have I been excessive? Too loud? Too invasive?*

Practice Taking Action

Recall that Protectors have a big, forceful energy that others often experience as excessive, or too much, even when Protectors are holding some of it back. Many Protectors are simply unaware that their impact may be overwhelming to others. Here is a practice:

> *Each day, I will make a conscious effort to moderate my urge to use direct action to express my desires and my sense of justice and truth.*
> *I will do my best to notice how the urge to express myself comes from my gut, from my body. I will contain my initial impulse to take direct action while I consider the possible consequences, and ask myself if a more moderate approach would be better.*

To check your progress, notice if you are respecting others' boundaries and positions or if you are inadvertently imposing your will on them. Remember that Protectors often take an all-or-nothing approach to relating to others, which makes it difficult for them to be moderate.

Practice Previewing and Reviewing Your Progress

Preview:

When you first get up in the morning, center yourself by practicing the breathing exercise for a few moments. Then say to yourself:

Today I will practice coming to each situation more open to others' different positions and different energy. I will practice being more aware and accepting of my own natural vulnerabilities and tender feelings. It is crucial that I recognize my denial of vulnerability and my own softer feelings, since this denial results in deeply embedded habits that don't serve me well.

When you do this practice, adopt the stance that the changes you are previewing are already true about you, since what you came to believe and the associated adaptive strategy basically are no longer true.

Review:

In the evening each day, take a few minutes to review your progress. Ask yourself, with an open mind and heart:

How did I do today in approaching each situation open to others' different positions and energy? How was I at accepting my own natural vulnerabilities and tender feelings? How did I do at noticing my impact on others?

Use what you learn from this review to guide your thoughts and actions for the next day's preview and review practice.

Working with the "4As" of Awareness, Acceptance, Action, and Adherence

You can do this practice a number of times each day, theoretically as often as you notice your reactivity. Note that the "4As" process is clearly embedded in this practice. It may help in doing this practice to use "I" instead of "you" statements. In committing to this practice, you virtually make life your mindfulness practice. Here is the practice:

When you get upset or reactive, *notice* that you are experiencing blocks to your sense of truth and justice and associated issues of power and control, all fueled by your big, excessive energy called lust.

Pause to *collect* back and *contain* the energy of your reactivity by breathing down into your belly.

Through *non-judgmental inquiry,* can you become aware that your reactivity comes from your core belief that to gain worth and respect and to not be taken advantage of you must be strong, powerful, and invulnerable and avoid becoming weak and powerless?

With *discernment* can you realize that this belief most likely is just an old habit of mind and gently coach yourself into *letting go,* realizing that your urge to take charge and impose your sense of justice is just your version of the truth and the way you protect yourself from being vulnerable, which to you means weak.

Can you also gently coach yourself into *action* that is respectful to yourself and others and through awareness apply force or energy befitting the situation? Let yourself be vulnerable to and affected by the experience of each person's truth and worth.

Remind yourself to notice and absorb that you are empowered by respecting boundaries, moderating your impact on others, and valuing others' views.

Practice Reflecting to Reclaim Your Higher Qualities

At least once a week, take a few minutes in a quiet place to reflect upon and contemplate both the fundamental principle and the ultimate task for Protectors. A natural outdoor setting is an ideal place to do this. Simply reflect on the following:

> *The* fundamental principle *that Protectors lose sight of and need to regain is that we are all initially without guile and that we can all sense the truth. Therefore, the* ultimate task *for Protectors is to reclaim the original innocence of coming to each situation without prejudging it or overpowering it and to realize that truth flows from universal laws, not from personal views. This ultimate task is more easily accomplished when you approach each situation with an appropriate energy, or force, and with an equal respect for yourself and others.*

Then explore what adopting these truths would mean to your life. You are likely to experience the more openhearted connections, heightened respect for all beings, and even abiding calm that naturally result from this practice.

Practices for the Mediator (Type Nine)

We recommend that you begin by choosing just one practice to work on before you move on to the others. It may take you a week or more with each practice to experience a sense of progress. You might find it helpful to keep a journal to record your daily responses to these practices. And you may want to record these practices so that you can listen to them as helpful reminders.

Practice Receptive Awareness

Pay particular attention to how much your attention and energy are pulled by and then dispersed into the many claims made upon you, leading to indecisiveness and over-accommodation. Stop several times a day for a minute or so to reflect by breathing down and in, allowing yourself to become aware and receptive. Then consider the following questions:

> *How have all the people and things around me been pulling at and competing for my attention? How indecisive have I been? In what ways have I gone along with others' agendas and plans? In what ways have I been sidetracked into focusing on secondary priorities or inessentials?*

Practice Taking Action

Recall that Mediators tend to have their attention pulled by everything around them, which allows them to blend in and feel a sense of belonging. This experience of belonging gives Mediators a sense of their importance, which serves as a substitute for their own real value and importance. Here is a practice:

> *Each day, I will make a conscious effort to place my attention on what is important to me and to use my energy for my own priorities, despite the discomfort or conflict that might arise from doing this.*
> *I will do my best to notice that I experience discomfort as uneasiness in my gut, and be aware that going along with others' agendas and diverting my attention to small pleasures or secondary tasks only reduces the discomfort temporarily. I will hold my ground, to acknowledge my importance as an individual, and to express myself accordingly.*

To check your progress, notice if you are following your own priorities and if this is helping to restore your sense of your importance as an individual. Evaluate how you are facing potential and actual situations of conflict or discomfort. Remember that Mediators tend to avoid conflict and to seek comfort as a strategy for coping with the belief that their own priorities and opinions are not important.

Practice Previewing and Reviewing Your Progress

Preview:

When you first get up in the morning, center yourself by practicing the breathing exercise for a few moments. Then say to yourself:

Today I will practice truly loving myself in ways equal to my love of others. I will practice appreciating my good qualities. When I need to make a decision, I will try to give my own opinion as much importance as the opinions of others. I can do this by setting my own personal priorities and by respecting my own limits and boundaries.

When you do this practice, adopt the stance that the changes you are previewing are already true about you, since what you came to believe and the associated adaptive strategy basically are no longer true.

Review:

In the evening each day, take a few minutes to review your progress. Ask yourself, with an open mind and heart:

In what ways did I express self-love and self-regard today? How did I respect my own limits and boundaries? How did I do in setting and carrying out my own personal priorities? Did I treat myself as being equally important as others?

Use what you learn from this review to guide your thoughts and actions for the next day's preview and review practice.

Working with the "4As" of Awareness, Acceptance, Action, and Adherence

You can do this practice a number of times each day, theoretically as often as you notice your reactivity. Note that the "4As" process is clearly embedded in this practice. It may help in doing this practice to use "I" instead of "you" statements. In committing to this practice, you virtually make life your mindfulness practice. Here is the practice:

When you get upset or reactive, *notice* that you are feeling pushed into action or conflict before you know what you want or need and that this feeling is fueled by an inertia toward self that causes you to forget your own priorities.

Pause to *collect* back and *contain* the energy of your reactivity by breathing down into your belly.

Through *non-judgmental inquiry,* can you become aware that your reactivity comes from your core belief that you aren't important or that you have to blend in and hence just go along and get along and avoid conflict in order to be of worth or importance?

With *discernment* can you realize that this belief most likely is just an old habit of mind and gently coach yourself into *letting go,* realizing that you need to love and value yourself just as much as you love and value all others?

Can you also gently coach yourself into *action* that is respectful to yourself and others and that takes into account your own priorities and importance as well as those of others? Let yourself honor your boundaries and limits.

Remind yourself to notice and absorb that you must be equally for yourself as well as for others in order to live in harmony and purpose.

Practice Reflecting to Reclaim Your Higher Qualities

At least once a week, take a few minutes in a quiet place to reflect upon and contemplate both the fundamental principle and the ultimate task for Mediators. A natural outdoor setting is an ideal place to do this. Simply reflect on the following:

The fundamental principle *that Mediators lose sight of and need to regain is that everyone belongs equally in a state of unconditional love and union. Therefore, the* ultimate task *for Mediators is to reclaim unconditional self-love and a sense of importance equal to that of others. This ultimate task is more easily accomplished when you pay attention to your own position and priorities and when you act in the ways that are essential to your own well-being as well as the well-being of others.*

Then explore what adopting these truths would mean to your life. You are likely to experience the newfound self-regard, freedom to express yourself, and love of life that naturally result from this practice.

Appendix A:
Additional Enneagram Resources

The resources listed here are from the Enneagram in the Narrative Tradition of Self-Discovery of Helen Palmer and David Daniels. Teaching and learning in this tradition involves using the panel interviewing method and the process of inquiry and elicitation, mindfulness practices, small group exercises, and lecture. This method embodies the principle of self-discovery as the first step in personal development. *The Essential Enneagram* is based on this principle of self-discovery. The Narrative Tradition makes it possible for all individuals to speak for themselves as they are to themselves.

Our Organization, Classes, and Trainings

Enneagram Worldwide and the Enneagram Professional Training Program
1442-A Walnut Street, Suite #75
Berkeley, CA 94709
E-mail: sales@enneagramworldwide.com
Phone: (866) 366–8973 (toll-free in the United States) or (513) 829–3457
San Francisco Bay Area phone: (510) 234–1600
Web site: www.Enneagramworldwide.com. Features hundreds of pages of content, including a concise introduction to the Enneagram and its value, the "Tour of the Types," all forty-five combinations of relationships, type and instinctual subtype determination, numerous products, and listing of programs, trainings, and classes.
Web site: www.Enneagram.com. Features Helen Palmer's online course, articles, teaching schedule, and a variety of products.

Books

These titles are available through www.enneagramworldwide.com or Amazon.com and at bookstores.
The Enneagram: Understanding Yourself and the Others in Your Life by Helen Palmer. San Francisco: HarperSanFrancisco, 1988.

The Enneagram in Love and Work by Helen Palmer. San Francisco: HarperSan-
Francisco, 1995.

The Pocket Enneagram by Helen Palmer. San Francisco: HarperSanFrancisco,
1995.

The Enneagram Advantage by Helen Palmer. New York: Harmony Books, 1998
(limited availability).

DVDs

These DVDs are available through www.ennegramworldwide.com.

Breaking Out of the Box: Discovering the Enneagram, developed for public television; featuring Helen Palmer; produced by Michael Schwarz, a premier
television producer. A vibrant and informative introduction.

*Nine Paths to a Productive and Fulfilling Life: A Comprehensive Overview of the
Enneagram* and *The Enneagram in the Workplace: Nine Paths to Effective Leadership and Performance,* featuring David Daniels and Courtney Behm. *Nine
Paths,* which is systematic, comprehensive and fast-moving, provides a fundamental introduction to the Enneagram with clips of exemplars, narra-
tion, graphics, and lectures. *The Enneagram in the Workplace* shows successful
business exemplars covering leadership themes and challenges. Includes
two 16-page Discussion Guides.

Men and Women in Relationship, produced by Helen Palmer, explores male
and female points of view in relationships, presents the ways in which
type shows up in relationships, and is ideal for showing the dimensions of
relationship.

Tour of the Types with Short Cuts, produced by Helen Palmer, presents exemplars of the types and discusses habitual patterns and themes; it also features
shortcut versions that are excellent for use in introductory classes.

Audios and CDs

These CDs are available through www.enneagramworldwide.com.

The Enneagram: Eight-Hour Introduction by Helen Palmer. Produced by Sounds
True Recordings.

*The Instinctual Subtypes: The Enneagram's Hidden Force: A Conversation with
David Daniels,* featuring Peter O'Hanrahan, and exemplars of the types.

Conversations with David: A periodic audio product featuring David Daniels
and special guests exploring a variety of key Enneagram types.

Organizations

Association of Enneagram Teachers in the Narrative Tradition (AET)
Teachers and participants in the Narrative Tradition trainings
P.O. Box 68

Topsfield, MA 01983
Web site: www.aetnt.com
E-mail: aetnt@juno.com

International Enneagram Association (IEA)
4100 Executive Park Drive, Suite 16
Cincinnati, OH 45241
Phone: (513) 232-5054
Web site: www.internationalenneagram.org

Newsletters/Periodicals

TALK Newsletter/Journal of the Association of Enneagram Teachers in the
    Narrative Tradition (AET)
101 Elizabeth Way
San Rafael, CA 94901
E-mail: SanLynCent@aol.com

Enneagram Monthly
748 Wayside Road
Portola Valley, CA 94082
Phone: (650) 851-4806
E-mail: editor@ennea.org

Appendix B:
Validity of the Essential Enneagram Test

We designed a simple paragraph test based on logical constructs of the nine Enneagram personality types derived from the theoretical work of Helen Palmer and David Daniels. Each paragraph includes:

- The overall worldview of the type
- The attentional style
- The dominant mental and emotional biases
- The central preoccupations
- The positive attributes of the type

We asked representatives of each personality type to review and revise their respective paragraphs to ensure that the paragraphs were congruent with their actual experience of being that type. We then reviewed their revisions to ensure that the paragraphs were accurate from a theoretical standpoint and were equally socially desirable.

We established the validity of the Essential Enneagram Test by testing 970 individuals throughout the United States who enrolled in Enneagram classes or volunteered for typing interviews. These individuals did not know their Enneagram personality type and were unfamiliar with the Enneagram. Sixty-five percent of the sample were women, and 35 percent were men.

We compared each individual's Essential Enneagram Test self-rating to one of two "gold standard" ratings:

- One of the gold standards used was a diagnostic typing interview conducted by a certified Enneagram teacher who did not know how the individuals had rated themselves.
- The other gold standard was the individual's own reevaluation on the Assessment Inventory after taking a ten-week Enneagram course or its equivalent.

The two gold standards produced similar results. These results confirm the validity of the Essential Enneagram Test—that is, the probability that users will accurately select their personality type from among the nine paragraphs.

We analyzed the results for each of the nine paragraphs separately. Each of the nine paragraphs, or personality types, has its own probability of being accurately distinguished among the nine Enneagram personality types. The Type Determination pages in *The Essential Enneagram* show the accuracy of each paragraph. For example, the Perfectionist paragraph has a 66 percent accuracy. This means that two-thirds of the people who selected the Perfectionist paragraph as their type were also identified as this type by the gold standard, either by an expert's rating through a structured interview or by their own reevaluation of themselves following an Enneagram course.

People sometimes choose a paragraph in the Essential Enneagram Test that is not their correct personality type but is one of the look-alike types associated with their personality type or is one of the four personality types connected to their personality type. For this reason, we also calculated the probability of individuals being each of the other eight types if their self-rating was not correct when compared to the gold standard. The Type Determination pages in *The Essential Enneagram* show these other analyses. For example, 8 percent of the subjects who chose the Perfectionist paragraph were actually the Romantic type, 8 percent were the Loyal Skeptic type, 7 percent were the Giver type, and 5 percent were the Mediator type. The remaining 6 percent of those who characterized themselves as Perfectionist were distributed among the remaining four types.

The Type Determination pages list the probability of the type that subjects chose being their correct type. They also list the probabilities of other types being subjects' correct type instead. The Type Determination pages include step-by-step instructions for testing the accuracy of one's choices. The overall pattern is a measure of validity based on the following statistical analyses.

We analyzed each Enneagram paragraph with respect to sensitivity, specificity, predictive value of positives, predictive value of negatives, test efficiency, and Cohen's Kappa test for intraclass correlation. We computed Kappa statistics for the test across all nine scales as a measure of overall test concordance. Test validity as measured by congruency of respondents' answers to the gold standard was statistically and clinically significant. The overall Kappa for the entire test was 0.5254 ($p < 0.0001$), considered a significant degree of concordance. All analyses of individual items exhibited concordance or intraclass correlations significant at $p < 0.0001$. We performed reliability analysis with a small naive group of graduate students ($n = 62$). We gave alternative versions of the inventory four weeks apart without an introduction to the Enneagram and without introducing any other bias. The analysis revealed a significant concordance, Kappa = 0.589 ($p < 0.0001$).